GACE Media Specialist

101
102
601

Teacher Certification Exam

By: Sharon A. Wynne, M.S.

XAMonline, INC.
Boston

Copyright © 2018 XAMonline, Inc.
All rights reserved. No part of the material protected by this copyright notice may be reproduced or utilized in any form or by any means, electronic or mechanical, including photocopying, recording or by any information storage and retrievable system, without written permission from the copyright holder.

To obtain permission(s) to use the material from this work for any purpose including workshops or seminars, please submit a written request to:

XAMonline, Inc.
21 Orient Avenue
Melrose, MA 02176
Toll Free 1-800-301-4647
Email: info@xamonline.com
Web www.xamonline.com

Library of Congress Cataloging-in-Publication Data

Wynne, Sharon A.
    GACE Media Specialist 101, 102, 601: Teacher Certification / Sharon A. Wynne.
    ISBN 978-1-64239-032-2
    1. Media Specialist 101, 102, 601   2. Study Guides.   3. GACE
    4. Teachers' Certification & Licensure.   5. Careers

Disclaimer:
The opinions expressed in this publication are the sole works of XAMonline and were created independently from the National Education Association, Educational Testing Service, or any State Department of Education, National Evaluation Systems or other testing affiliates.

Between the time of publication and printing, state specific standards as well as testing formats and website information may change that is not included in part or in whole within this product. Sample test questions are developed by XAMonline and reflect similar content as on real tests; however, they are not former tests. XAMonline assembles content that aligns with state standards but makes no claims nor guarantees teacher candidates a passing score. Numerical scores are determined by testing companies such as NES or ETS and then are compared with individual state standards. A passing score varies from state to state.

Printed in the United States of America   œ-1

GACE: Media Specialist 101, 102, 601
ISBN: 978-1-64239-032-2

TEACHER CERTIFICATION STUDY GUIDE

Table of Contents

SUBAREA I.   **INFORMATION ACCESS AND DELIVERY IN THE LIBRARY MEDIA PROGRAM**

COMPETENCY 1.0   **UNDERSTAND THE MISSION OF THE LIBRARY MEDIA PROGRAM AND THE ROLES AND RESPONSIBILITIES OF THE MEDIA SPECIALIST**... 1

Skill 1.1   Identifying characteristics and functions of an effective school library media program... 1

Skill 1.2   Recognizing the mission of the library media program in providing equitable physical and intellectual access to information, ideas, and learning and teaching tools.. 2

Skill 1.3   Recognizing the importance of creating an environment that supports multiple uses of the library media center and promotes lifelong learning 3

Skill 1.4   Demonstrating knowledge of management functions of the media specialist 3

Skill 1.5   Recognizing the roles and responsibilities of the media specialist in providing expertise in the use of information resources and technology and in serving as a resource person for members of the learning community 4

Skill 1.6   Applying knowledge of strategies for encouraging students to take responsibility for their own learning 5

COMPETENCY 2.0   **UNDERSTAND THE CHARACTERISTICS OF EFFICIENT AND ETHICAL INFORMATION-SEEKING BEHAVIOR BY ALL MEMBERS OF THE LEARNING COMMUNITY**... 6

Skill 2.1   Applying knowledge of strategies for locating, critically evaluating and using information in a variety of formats for given purposes..... 6

Skill 2.2   Recognizing strategies for developing library media services that include print, nonprint and electronic resources that address the learning abilities, styles and needs of all users............................... 7

MEDIA SPECIALIST

Skill 2.3	Demonstrating knowledge of strategies for creating and communicating policies and procedures that reflect the legal guidelines and professional ethics of librarianship	9
Skill 2.4	Identifying strategies that promote the responsible use of information and information technology	10
Skill 2.5	Demonstrating knowledge of issues related to the effective use of current, relevant information processes and resources, including emerging technologies	12

COMPETENCY 3.0 UNDERSTAND CHARACTERISTICS OF LITERATURE FOR CHILDREN AND YOUNG ADULTS AND STRATEGIES FOR PROMOTING LITERACY 15

Skill 3.1	Demonstrating knowledge of historical and contemporary trends and multicultural issues in reading material for children and young adults	15
Skill 3.2	Demonstrating knowledge of strategies for collaborating with teachers to integrate literature into the curriculum	19
Skill 3.3	Demonstrating knowledge of issues related to the selection and recommendation of literature for a school library media program	20
Skill 3.4	Demonstrating knowledge of how to use literacy research to select literature that facilitates the reading process and develops fluency in readers	21
Skill 3.5	Identifying strategies for developing a sense of appreciation for literature in others and for promoting the habit of lifelong reading	22

COMPETENCY 4.0 UNDERSTAND STRATEGIES FOR PROVIDING ACCESS TO INFORMATION, IDEAS AND LITERATURE 24

Skill 4.1	Identifying relationships among facilities, programs and environment that affect student learning	24
Skill 4.2	Demonstrating knowledge of practices that support flexible, open access for the library media center resources and services for classes, small groups and individuals	24

Skill 4.3	Recognizing factors involved in the physical design and furnishing of a flexible, functional and barrier-free library media center	25
Skill 4.4	Demonstrating knowledge of elements of design to consider in promoting efficient and appropriate use of the library media center	28
Skill 4.5	Demonstrating knowledge of collaborative techniques for creating and maintaining an attractive, positive climate in a technologically rich, student-centered library media center	29
Skill 4.6	Identifying methods for using research-based data, including action research, to improve the library media program	29
Skill 4.7	Recognizing organizational structures that enhance or impede physical or intellectual access to ideas and information	33

SUBAREA II. INFORMATION LITERACY SKILLS

COMPETENCY 5.0	UNDERSTAND INFORMATION RESOURCES AND STRATEGIES FOR LOCATING AND ACCESSING INFORMATION RESOURCES FOR A PARTICULAR PURPOSE	34
Skill 5.1	Identifying types, characteristics and uses of various print, nonprint and electronic information resources	34
Skill 5.2	Recognizing and comparing the advantages and limitations of various information resources, formats and services	35
Skill 5.3	Demonstrating knowledge of strategies for locating specific information in various types of resources and applying criteria for selecting an appropriate resource for locating specific information	36
Skill 5.4	Demonstrating knowledge of methods for conducting print-based and electronic searches, for evaluating the progress of a search, and for adjusting search strategies in response to search results	37
Skill 5.5	Identifying strategies for helping students learn methods to locate and access information efficiently and independently	38

TEACHER CERTIFICATION STUDY GUIDE

COMPETENCY 6.0 UNDERSTAND STRATEGIES FOR EVALUATING INFORMATION AND COMMUNICATING INFORMATION OBTAINED FROM A SEARCH 41

Skill 6.1 Identifying strategies for locating potentially useful information and applying criteria for evaluating information 41

Skill 6.2 Demonstrating knowledge of strategies for summarizing, organizing and synthesizing information and for drawing appropriate conclusions 42

Skill 6.3 Demonstrating knowledge of strategies for presenting information in a form that communicates clearly what has been learned 42

Skill 6.4 Demonstrating knowledge of considerations in selecting an appropriate format to communicate information 43

Skill 6.5 Applying knowledge of guidelines for preparing a bibliography or other necessary documentation 44

Skill 6.6 Identifying strategies for helping students learn how to evaluate information and for helping students adopt effective and creative approaches to communicating information 45

COMPETENCY 7.0 UNDERSTAND METHODS AND MATERIALS FOR PROMOTING LEARNING AND INFORMATION LITERACY SKILLS 46

Skill 7.1 Demonstrating familiarity with human development, learning theory and instructional design in relation to teaching information literacy skills 46

Skill 7.2 Demonstrating knowledge of methods for assessing learner needs, instructional methodologies and information processes 47

Skill 7.3 Demonstrating knowledge of methods for designing information skills instruction that is based on student interest and learning needs that are linked to the goal of student achievement 48

Skill 7.4 Identifying techniques of incorporating authentic learning opportunities into the library media program 49

Skill 7.5 Demonstrating knowledge of various teaching strategies and activities for encouraging critical and creative thinking by promoting information literacy skills, including reading, listening and viewing 50

MEDIA SPECIALIST

TEACHER CERTIFICATION STUDY GUIDE

Skill 7.6 Recognizing techniques for creating instructional materials that encourage student learning and reading 51

COMPETENCY 8.0 UNDERSTAND THE CHARACTERISTICS OF EFFECTIVE TEACHERS OF INFORMATION LITERACY SKILLS 53

Skill 8.1 Identifying strategies for working in partnership with classroom teachers and other educators to plan, deliver and evaluate information skills instruction 53

Skill 8.2 Applying knowledge of the advantages and limitations of various instructional strategies and assessment tools for given educational goals or objectives 53

Skill 8.3 Demonstrating knowledge of strategies for encouraging students to use information skills to solve problems, pursue knowledge and explore the world of information for personal interest and self-improvement 55

Skill 8.4 Applying knowledge of strategies for selecting resources, including technological resources, to support students with diverse learning abilities, styles and needs 55

Skill 8.5 Recognizing methods for maintaining regular communication between the school library media center and students, their families and the community 56

Skill 8.6 Recognizing the benefits of self-reflection as a path to professional growth 57

SUBAREA III. COLLABORATION AND LEADERSHIP IN THE LIBRARY MEDIA CONTEXT

COMPETENCY 9.0 UNDERSTAND THE ROLE OF THE MEDIA SPECIALIST IN CURRICULUM DEVELOPMENT 58

Skill 9.1 Demonstrating knowledge of basic principles of curriculum development and standardized practices 58

Skill 9.2 Recognizing the importance of participating in district, building, departmental and grade level curriculum design and assessment projects 59

Skill 9.3	Identifying strategies for engaging in cooperative planning with faculty and others to ensure that information literacy skills are integrated into the curriculum	59
Skill 9.4	Recognizing methods for collaborating with classroom teachers to promote interdisciplinary learning	60
Skill 9.5	Applying knowledge of methods for collaborating with staff in selecting and acquiring resources to support curricular needs	60
Skill 9.6	Applying knowledge of academic performance standards in selecting and acquiring resources to support curricular needs	61

COMPETENCY 10.0   UNDERSTAND THE ROLE OF THE MEDIA SPECIALIST AS AN INSTRUCTIONAL PARTNER 62

Skill 10.1	Demonstrating knowledge of current trends and issues in education and of research indicating the relationship between the school library media program and improved student achievement	62
Skill 10.2	Demonstrating knowledge of techniques for collaborating with teachers in the development of instructional strategies, activities and assessments to guide students in developing a full range of information literacy and communication abilities	63
Skill 10.3	Demonstrating knowledge of methods and materials for instructing and training members of the school learning community in the use of information resources and technologies	63
Skill 10.4	Identifying strategies for working with members of the learning community to share information, engage in action research and apply research results	64

COMPETENCY 11.0   UNDERSTAND THE ROLE OF THE MEDIA SPECIALIST AS AN EDUCATIONAL LEADER 65

Skill 11.1	Demonstrating basic knowledge of leadership strategies, expectations and goals	65
Skill 11.2	Recognizing the role of the media specialist in providing leadership and expertise in the use of learning resources and instructional technology	66
Skill 11.3	Identifying strategies for promoting a culture of inquiry within the school community	67

Skill 11.4 Demonstrating knowledge of methods for using the school's mission, goals, policies, structure and culture to advocate for the school library media program 68

Skill 11.5 Demonstrating knowledge of strategies for establishing partnerships with members of the school community to incorporate the library media program into school improvement activities 74

COMPETENCY 12.0 UNDERSTAND THE RELATIONSHIP BETWEEN THE LIBRARY MEDIA PROGRAM AND INFORMATION RESOURCES BEYOND THE SCHOOL 75

Skill 12.1 Recognizing the role of the library media program in connecting the school community to local, district, state, national and global resources...75

Skill 12.2 Recognizing methods for establishing and maintaining connections between the school community and the larger library community for the purposes of resource sharing, networking and developing common policies and procedures...76

Skill 12.3 Demonstrating knowledge of techniques for interacting with other professionals at a variety of institutions..77

Skill 12.4 Demonstrating knowledge of methods for helping members of the school community locate, access and evaluate information resources beyond the school library media center 78

Skill 12.5 Recognizing the role of professional associations and journals in maintaining current, research-based knowledge about information resources and technologies..79

SUBAREA IV. LIBRARY MEDIA PROGRAM ADMINISTRATION

COMPETENCY 13.0 UNDERSTAND PRINCIPLES AND PRACTICES FOR MANAGING LIBRARY MEDIA INFORMATION RESOURCES..81

Skill 13.1 Demonstrating knowledge of strategies for selecting, analyzing and evaluating library media collections to develop a collection that supports the needs of a diverse population 81

Skill 13.2 Identifying strategies for involving the learning community in the evaluation, selection and deselection of library media information resources..84

Skill 13.3	Identifying and applying standard procedures for classifying and cataloging library media information resources	86
Skill 13.4	Identifying practices and policies that ensure flexible and equitable access to facilities and resources based on users' needs	87
Skill 13.5	Demonstrating knowledge of the role of technology in the organization, management and circulation of resources	88
COMPETENCY 14.0	**UNDERSTAND PRINCIPLES AND PRACTICES RELATED TO THE MANAGEMENT OF TECHNOLOGICAL RESOURCES OF THE LIBRARY MEDIA PROGRAM**	**90**
Skill 14.1	Recognizing and comparing the advantages and limitations of various technological resources, formats and services	90
Skill 14.2	Applying knowledge of criteria for selecting and managing existing and emerging technological applications, materials, services and formats to support and enhance the curriculum	91
Skill 14.3	Demonstrating knowledge of strategies for providing support and training to the learning community in the use of technological resources	92
Skill 14.4	Applying knowledge of strategies for coordinating the use of technological resources with administrators, faculty and staff	93
COMPETENCY 15.0	**UNDERSTAND PRINCIPLES AND PRACTICES RELATED TO THE MANAGEMENT OF HUMAN, FINANCIAL AND PHYSICAL RESOURCES OF THE LIBRARY MEDIA PROGRAM**	**94**
Skill 15.1	Recognizing methods of developing and evaluating policies and procedures that support the mission of the school and address the specific needs of the library media program	94
Skill 15.2	Identifying strategies for communicating the status and needs of the library media program to the larger learning community and for advocating for ongoing administrative support for the library media program	95
Skill 15.3	Demonstrating knowledge of accepted management principles and practices for the selection, supervision, training and evaluation of library media staff and volunteers	96

Skill 15.4   Identifying types, characteristics and uses of financial budgets and reports and demonstrating basic knowledge of funding sources for library media programs 98

Skill 15.5   Demonstrating knowledge of issues related to running a library media program within a budget 100

COMPETENCY 16.0   UNDERSTAND THE COMPREHENSIVE AND COLLABORATIVE   NATURE OF STRATEGIC PLANNING AND ASSESSMENT FOR THE LIBRARY MEDIA PROGRAM……………………………………..102

Skill 16.1   Demonstrating knowledge of strategies for collaborating with teachers, administrators, students and others in the learning community to develop, implement and assess long term strategic plans for the library media program 102

Skill 16.2   Identifying strategies for aligning the resources and services of the library media program with information literacy standards and with the school's goals, objectives and standards 103

Skill 16.3   Recognizing methods for evaluating the effectiveness of policies, procedures and operations of a library media program and for modifying the library media program based on evaluation results 103

Skill 16.4   Applying knowledge of procedures for collecting and analyzing relevant quantitative and qualitative data regarding user needs to make decisions with regard to the library media program 105

Resources 108

Sample Test 119

Answer Key 146

Rigor Table 147

Rationales with Sample Questions 148

TEACHER CERTIFICATION STUDY GUIDE

Great Study and Testing Tips!

The focus of this study guide is to reinforce *what* you should study in order to prepare for the subject assessment, but equally important is *how* you study.

You can increase your chances of truly mastering the information by taking some simple, but effective steps.

Study Tips:

1. Some foods aid the learning process. Foods such as milk, nuts, seeds, rice and oats help your study efforts by releasing natural memory enhancers called CCKs (*cholecystokinin*) composed of *tryptophan*, *choline* and *phenylalanine*. All of these chemicals enhance the neurotransmitters associated with memory. Before studying, try a light, protein-rich meal of eggs, turkey and fish. All of these foods release the memory enhancing chemicals. The better the connections, the more you comprehend.

Likewise, before you take a test, stick to a light snack of energy boosting and relaxing foods. A glass of milk, a piece of fruit, or some peanuts all release various memory-boosting chemicals and help you to relax and focus on the subject at hand.

2. Learn to take great notes. A by-product of our modern culture is that we have grown accustomed to getting our information in short doses (i.e., TV news sound bites or USA Today style newspaper articles.)

Consequently, we've subconsciously trained ourselves to assimilate information better in neat little packages. If your notes are scrawled all over the paper, they fragment the flow of the information. Instead, strive for clarity. Newspapers use a standard format to achieve clarity. Your notes can be much clearer through use of proper formatting. A very effective format is called the *"Cornell Method."*

> Take a sheet of lined, loose-leaf notebook paper and draw a line all the way down the paper about 1-2" from the left-hand edge.

> Draw another line across the width of the paper about 1-2" up from the bottom. Repeat this process on the reverse side of the page.

Look at the highly effective result. You have ample room for notes, a left hand margin for special emphasis items or inserting supplementary data from the textbook, a large area at the bottom for a brief summary, and a little rectangular space for just about anything you want.

MEDIA SPECIALIST

3. Get the concept then the details. Too often we focus on the details and don't gather an understanding of the concept. However, if you simply memorize only dates, places or names, you may well miss the whole point of the subject.

A key way to understand ideas is to put them in your own words. If you are working from a textbook, automatically summarize each paragraph in your mind. If you are outlining text, don't simply copy the author's words.

Instead, *rephrase* them in your own words. You remember your own thoughts and words much better than someone else's, and you subconsciously tend to associate the important details to the core concepts.

4. Ask Why? Pull apart written material paragraph by paragraph, and don't forget the captions under the illustrations.

Example: If the heading is "Stream Erosion", flip it around to read "Why do streams erode?" Then answer the questions.

If you train your mind to think in a series of questions and answers, not only will you learn more, but you will also lessen the test anxiety because you will be used to answering questions.

5. Read for reinforcement and future needs. Even if you only have 10 minutes, put your notes or a book in your hand. Your mind is similar to a computer; you have to input data in order to have it processed. *By reading, you are creating the neural connections for future retrieval.* The more times you read something, the more you reinforce the learning of ideas.

Even if you don't fully understand something on the first pass, *your mind stores much of the material for later recall.*

6. Relax to learn. Go into exile. Our bodies respond to an inner clock called biorhythms. Burning the midnight oil works well for some people, but not everyone.

If possible, set aside a particular place to study that is free of distractions. Shut off the television, cell phone and pager, and exile your friends and family during your study period.

If you really are bothered by silence, try background music. Light classical music at a low volume has been shown to aid in concentration over other types. Music that evokes pleasant emotions without lyrics is highly suggested. Try just about anything by Mozart. His work will relax you.

7. Use arrows not highlighters. At best, it's difficult to read a page full of yellow, pink, blue and green streaks. Try staring at a neon sign for a while and you'll soon see that the horde of colors obscure the message.

A quick note, a brief dash of color, an underline and an arrow pointing to a particular passage is much clearer than a horde of highlighted words.

8. Budget your study time. Although you shouldn't ignore any of the material, *allocate your available study time in the same ratio that topics may appear on the test.*

TEACHER CERTIFICATION STUDY GUIDE

Testing Tips:

1. Get smart, play dumb. Don't read anything into the question. Don't make an assumption that the test writer is looking for something else than what is asked. Stick to the question as written and don't read extra things into it.

2. Read the question and all the choices *twice* before answering the question. You may miss something by not carefully reading, and then re-reading both the question and the answers.

If you really don't have a clue as to the right answer, leave it blank on the first time through. Go on to the other questions, as they may provide a clue as to how to answer the skipped questions.

If later on, you still can't answer the skipped ones . . . *Guess.* The only penalty for guessing is that you *might* get it wrong. Only one thing is certain; if you don't put anything down, you will get it wrong!

3. Turn the question into a statement. Look at the way the questions are worded. The syntax of the question usually provides a clue. Does it seem more familiar as a statement rather than as a question? Does it sound strange?

By turning a question into a statement, you may be able to spot if an answer sounds right, and it may also trigger memories of material you have read.

4. Look for hidden clues. It's actually very difficult to compose multiple-foil (choice) questions without giving away part of the answer in the options presented.

In most multiple-choice questions you can often readily eliminate one or two of the potential answers. This leaves you with only two real possibilities, and automatically your odds go to Fifty-Fifty for very little work.

5. Trust your instincts. For every fact that you have read, you subconsciously retain something of that knowledge. On questions that you aren't really certain about, go with your basic instincts. **Your first impression on how to answer a question is usually correct.**

6. Mark your answers directly on the test booklet. Don't bother trying to fill in the optical scan sheet on the first pass through the test.

Just be very careful not to miss-mark your answers when you eventually transcribe them to the scan sheet.

7. Watch the clock! You have a set amount of time to answer the questions. Don't get bogged down trying to answer a single question at the expense of 10 questions you can more readily answer.

TEACHER CERTIFICATION STUDY GUIDE

SUBAREA I.	INFORMATION ACCESS AND DELIVERY IN THE LIBRARY MEDIA PROGRAM

COMPETENCY 1.0   UNDERSTAND THE MISSION OF THE LIBRARY MEDIA PROGRAM AND THE ROLES AND RESPONSIBILITIES OF THE MEDIA SPECIALIST.

Skill 1.1   Identifying characteristics and functions of an effective school library media program

An effective school library media program can become the heart of learning in any school environment. A deciding factor in the success of the program is the dedication of the school library media specialist. For a school library media program to be successful it must possess the following characteristics:

- The program must be student-centered. Students have the opportunity to learn to be efficient managers of information. They participate in learning activities that foster creativity and build critical thinking skills. Students collaborate with the school library media specialists to facilitate their learning experiences.
- The program works to expand students' interests and to foster a love of reading, listening and viewing
- It works to provide access to information and assist students in evaluating that information so that it can be used effectively.
- The program assists students in becoming lifelong learners by teaching them to appreciate varying perspectives, act responsibly with regard to information, build critical thinking skills, analyze information and create products based upon the information learned.
- The school library media specialist collaborates with students and staff to provide authentic learning experiences that integrate information skills into the curriculum. Collaboration is one of the most crucial components to the success of a school library media program.
- The school library media specialist works as a leader within the school, bringing resources into the school and training others to use those resources.
- The school library media specialist creates partnerships within the community, further enhancing educational opportunities for students.
- The school library media specialist provides physical access to resources that meets the needs of all populations.

Skill 1.2   Recognizing the mission of the library media program in providing equitable physical and intellectual access to information, ideas, and learning and teaching tools

The mission of any organization, business or educational institution should evolve from the needs and expectations of its customers. In the case of the school library media center, its mission must parallel the school's mission and attend to the users' needs for resources and services.

The school library media program should examine the following school and student characteristics.

School:

- The mission of the school library media center should reflect and harmonize with the stated school mission.
- The program's mission should reflect the academic, vocational and compensatory directions of the school curriculum.
- The mission should reflect the willingness of the administration and faculty to support the program.

Student:

- The mission is influenced by pupil demographics: age, achievement, ability levels, reading levels and learning styles.
- The mission may indicate student interest in self-directed learning and exploratory reading.
- The mission reflects support from parents and community groups.

Information Power: Guidelines for School Library Media Programs (1988) and *Information Power: Building Partnerships for Learning* (1998) state that the mission of a library media program should focus upon these items.

- Ensuring all patrons have intellectual access to information. The collection should contain a variety of resources on a wide range of topics. Patrons should be taught how to locate and utilize the information effectively.
- All patrons should have physical access to information. The collection should be well organized and should include resources that can be accessed both in and outside of the school.
- The media specialist should provide authentic learning experiences that enhance student levels of information literacy.
- The media specialist should work closely with teachers to provide activities that focus on lifelong learning.

Skill 1.3 Recognizing the importance of creating an environment that supports multiple uses of the library media center and promotes lifelong learning

A student-centered media center begins with providing access to resources in an environment that is both interesting and inviting. The space should be well-organized and clearly labeled so that resources can be located. It should have a welcoming atmosphere that entices students and staff to come to the media center to learn.

The school library media specialist is crucial to the development of a climate that encourages learning. To provide such as atmosphere the school library media specialist must be willing to:

- promote the program as a wonderful place for learning,
- arrange materials so that they are easy to locate,
- set flexible schedules that allow for just in time learning,
- be eager to work with students and staff,
- maintain an attractive and inviting space,
- and collaborate with school staff and students.

Skill 1.4 Demonstrating knowledge of management functions of the media specialist

The American Association of School Librarians (AASL) and the Association for Educational Communications Technology (AECT) recommend that a school library media center is maintained by a licensed school library media specialist with a Master's degree from an educational program accredited by the American Library Association (ALA) or National Council for the Accreditation of Teacher Education (NCATE). This specialist should also receive qualified support staff.

The school library media specialist must demonstrate strong management skills. They are responsible for developing program goals, developing collections, managing the budget, consulting with teachers about using existing resources or producing new materials, providing student instruction and staff development, and overseeing the paraprofessional and nonprofessional staffs. It takes great effort to coordinate all of pieces to create a great school library media program.

The following summarizes AASL/AECT guidelines. The role of the school library media specialist is three-fold. The information specialist meets program needs by providing the following.

1. Access to the facility and materials that is non-restrictive—whether economically, ethnically or physically.
2. Communication to teachers, students, administrators and parents concerning new materials, services or technologies.
3. Efficient retrieval and information sharing systems.

The teacher specialist is charged with the following responsibilities.

1. Integrating information skills into the content curriculum.
2. Providing access to technology and instruction in its use.
3. Planning jointly with classroom teachers for the use and production of media appropriate to learner needs.
4. Using various instructional methods to provide staff development in policies, procedures, media production and technology use.

The instructional consultant uses expertise for the ensuing roles.

1. Participating in curriculum development and assessment.
2. Assisting teachers in acquiring information skills which they can incorporate into classroom instruction.
3. Designing a scope and sequence of teaching information skills.
4. Providing leadership in the use and assessment of information technologies.

In addition to the AASL/AECT guidelines also endorsed by the NEA, guidelines are available from state departments of education.

Skill 1.5 **Recognizing the roles and responsibilities of the media specialist in providing expertise in the use of information resources and technology and in serving as a resource person for members of the learning community**

School library media specialists play an essential role in the training for and use of technology resources. Their leadership and expertise is invaluable to a school's climate. It is imperative that media specialists stay abreast of emerging technologies and their impact on student achievement.

In this role, the media specialist is responsible for:
- assisting teachers with planning activities that integrate technology with the Quality Core Curriculum Standards and Resources (QCC),
- assisting with the use of technology as a tool,
- collaborating with teachers to select the appropriate technology to support instructional activities,
- teaching staff and students to use and evaluate information,
- providing a wide array of resources and opportunities for technology both on and offline,
- training teachers to use the technology tools available,
- providing leadership in the selection and evaluation of technology resources.

Skill 1.6 Applying knowledge of strategies for encouraging students to take responsibility for their own learning

The media specialist plays a key role in teaching students to master information literacy skills. When students are information literate, they can begin to take responsibility for their own learning.

Students need to be able to search for information on a wide array of topics for both school and personal reasons. The media specialist must teach students how to locate information through various resources. It is important for students to be taught effective search strategies for both print and electronic resources.

Independent learners need to be able to evaluate the information they locate. By teaching students how to evaluate print and non-print resources for their effectiveness students can best judge the accuracy of content.

Finally, students should be able to compile the information they gather into a product either for school or personal use. Students need to be taught note-taking skills along with the guidelines for copyright and fair use. They should also be taught how to write a research paper and how to use technology to present information.

When students have mastered information literacy skills they are better able determine their own needs and how to compile the information into a product they can use.

COMPETENCY 2.0 UNDERSTAND THE CHARACTERISTICS OF EFFICIENT AND ETHICAL INFORMATION-SEEKING BEHAVIOR BY ALL MEMBERS OF THE LEARNING COMMUNITY

Skill 2.1 Applying knowledge of strategies for locating, critically evaluating and using information in a variety of formats for given purposes

As students begin to form a topic, it is necessary for them to understand strategies that will make their search more effective and efficient. When searching for information the researcher should begin by writing down words or phrases that directly relate to the topic being covered. Researchers should start with general terms and break them down into more specific areas. These terms become the keywords that will be used in the search. A keyword is an important word or phrase that is used to retrieve information. Once the set of keywords has been determined, use these keywords to search books, articles, or electronic resources.

When searching through print materials the researcher will look for specific subject headings. Subject headings are words or phrases that are used to locate resources by topics. When information can be found under more than one subject heading the information is often cross-referenced. The words "See also" may be used to direct the researcher to a more appropriate heading. When using print references it can be helpful to consult an index to locate the keyword or any cross-referenced topics.

Electronic resources offer a wider array of strategies for locating information. Two of the most common strategies can be explained as follows:

- **Boolean operators**. Popular operators include:
  - AND – e.g. Lions AND tigers – commands the search engine to find both words in the searched text.
  - AND – e.g. Lions AND tigers – commands the search engine to find both words in the searched text.
  - AND NOT – e.g. Lions AND NOT tigers – commands the search engine to find texts that list lions but to ignore texts that list tigers.
  - OR – e.g. Lions OR tigers – commands the search engine top find texts that contain either word.
- **Wildcards** are an effective tool if one is unsure of the spelling or date for the topic being searched. An example would include the search for a list of all names in a database beginning with the letters ph. One way to phrase the search is to type "PH*". The asterisk at the end will cause the search to return anything in the database that begins with the letters "PH".

TEACHER CERTIFICATION STUDY GUIDE

As students begin to search for information resources for research or other projects it is important to evaluate the effectiveness of the selected resources.

There are several key factors to consider when looking at resources ranging from books to web pages.

These criteria include:
1. Audience: Who was this information intended to reach? What is the level of the information?
2. Scope: How detailed is the information? Is this work focused on an overall outline of the topic or does it provide in depth information on one specific aspect of the topic?
3. When was the information published? How often is the website updated?
4. Who is the author? What authority does this person have to be writing this article?
5. Is the article free from bias? Is it from a single person or an organization trying to argue for a certain position?
6. Does the author include a resource bibliography?
7. Does the information come from a scholarly source or from a popular source?

Skill 2.2　Recognizing strategies for developing library media services that include print, non-print and electronic resources that address the learning abilities, styles and needs of all users

Whether developing media services or building a collection of resources there are key factors that must be taken into consideration.

1. Knowledge of the existing collection or the ability to create a new collection.
2. Knowledge of the external environment (the school and community).
3. Assessment of school programs and user needs.
4. Development of overall policies and procedures.
5. Guidelines for specific selection decisions.
6. Evaluation criteria.
7. Establishment of a process for planning and implementing the collection plan.
8. Establishment of acquisition policies and procedures.
9. Establishment of maintenance program.
10. Establishment of procedures for evaluating the collection.

Once you have a plan, there are several procedures for implementing this plan.

1. Learn the collection. When a library medial specialist is new to a school with an existing collection, he or she should use several approaches to become familiar with the collection.
    a. Browse the shelves. Note your degree of familiarity with titles. Examine items that are unfamiliar to you. Determine the relationship between the materials on similar subjects in different formats. As you browse, include the reference and professional collections. Consider the accessibility of various media and the ease with which they can be located by users.
    b. Locate the center's procedures manual. Determine explanations for any irregularities that you perceive in the collection.
    c. Determine if any portions of the collection are housed in areas outside the media center.

   If the library media specialist is required to create a new collection, he or she should:
    a. Consult with the district director about new school collection policies.
    b. Examine the collections of other comparable schools.
    c. Examine companies, like Baker and Taylor's, who establish new collections based on criteria provided by the school.
2. Learn about the community.
    a. Examine the relationship of the media center to the total school program and other information agencies.
    b. Become familiar with the school, cultural, economic and political characteristics of the community and their influence on the schools.
3. Study the school's curriculum and the needs of all the users, including students and faculty. Examine the proportions of basic skills to enrichment offerings, academic or vocational courses, and requirements and electives. Determine the ability levels and grouping techniques for learners. Determine instructional objectives of teachers in various content areas or grade levels.
4. Examine existing policies and procedures for correlation to data acquired in researching the school and community.
5. Examine specific selection procedures to determine if guidelines are best met.
6. Examine evaluation criteria for effectiveness in maintaining an appropriate collection.
7. Examine the process to determine that accurate procedures are in place to meet the criteria.
8. Examine the acquisition plan. Determine the procedure by which materials are ordered, received, paid for and processed.
9. Examine maintenance procedures for repairing or replacing materials and equipment, replacing consumables and discarding non-repairable items.

10. Examine the policies and procedures for evaluation, and then examine the collection itself to determine if policies and procedures are contributing to quality and quantity.

Skill 2.3   Demonstrating knowledge of strategies for creating and communicating policies and procedures that reflect the legal guidelines and professional ethics of librarianship (e.g., user confidentiality and privacy, intellectual freedom)

The most efficient method of communicating policies and procedures to the faculty is the library media procedures manual. This manual should first present the library's mission and long-range objectives and then the specific policies designed to meet these objectives. The manual should include procedures for scheduling the facility, circulating materials and equipment, requesting consultation or instruction, and requesting media production.

Communicating policies to students is best facilitated by a structured orientation program and frequent visits to the media center to practice applying the procedures. In schools with closed circuit television, a live or taped program concerning library media use can be very successful.

Copyright and intellectual freedom issues may require additional attention. Specific activities incorporated into the creation of curriculum and research projects can be effective. Informational posters placed in strategic locations may be helpful in stressing the importance of following copyright guidelines.

Skill 2.4 **Identifying strategies that promote the responsible use of information and information technology (e.g., following intellectual property and copyright laws)**

Educators have the benefit of greater leeway in copying than any other group. Many print instructional materials carry statements that allow production of multiple copies for classroom use, provided they adhere to the "Guidelines for Classroom Copying in Nonprofit Educational Institutions." Teachers may duplicate enough copies to provide one per student per course provided that they meet the tests of brevity, spontaneity and cumulative effect.

1. Brevity test:
   Poetry - suggested maximum 250 words.
   Prose - one complete essay, story or article less than 2500 words or excerpts of no more than 1000 words or 10% of the work, depending on whichever is less. (Children's books with text under 2500 words may not be copied in their entirety. No more than two pages containing 10% of the text may be copied.)
   Illustration - charts, drawings, cartoons, etc. are limited to one per book or periodical article.
2. Spontaneity test: Normally copying that does not fall under the brevity test requires the publisher's permission for duplication. However, allowances are made if "the inspiration and decision to use the work" occurs too soon prior to classroom use for permission to be sought in writing.
3. Cumulative effect test: Even in the case of short poems or prose, it is preferable to make only one copy. However, three short items from one work are allowable during one class term. Reuse of copied material from term to term is expressly forbidden. Compilation of works into anthologies to be used in place of purchasing texts is prohibited.

Copyright legislation has existed in the United States for more than 100 years. Conflicts over copyright were settled in the courts. The 1976 Copyright Act, especially section 107 dealing with Fair Use, created legislative criteria to follow based on judicial precedents. In 1978, when the law took effect, it set regulations for duration and scope of copyright, specified author rights, and set monetary penalties for infringement.

The statutory penalty may be waived by the court for an employee of a non-profit educational institution where the employee can prove fair use intent.

Fair use, especially important to educators, is meant to create a balance between copyright protection and the needs of learners for access to protected material. Fair use is judged by the purpose of the use, the nature of the work (whether creative or informational), the quantity of the work for use and the market effect.

In essence, if a portion of a work is used to benefit the learner with no intent to deprive the author of his profits, fair use is granted. Recently, fair use has been challenged most in cases concerning the videotaping of television programs. Basic guidelines for this include showing the program within 10 days of recording and erasing the tape by the 45th day. Specific guidelines that affect copying audio-visual materials and computer software are too numerous to delineate. Most distributors place written regulations in the packaging of these products. Allowances for single back-up copies in the event of damage to the original are granted.

Computer software presents additional challenges with respect to copyright and fair use. Permissions, rights and restrictions for software, such as the number of computers where the software can be loaded, are listed in the form of a license.

Section 108 of the 1976 Copyright Act is pertinent to libraries in that it permits reproducing a single copy of an entire work if no financial gain is derived, if the library is public or archival, and if the copyright notice appears on all copies.

In any event in which violation of the law is a concern, the safest course of action is to seek written permission from the publisher of the copyrighted work. If permission is granted, a copy of that permission should accompany any duplicates.

When a suspected infringement of copyright is brought to the attention of the school library media specialist, he or she should follow certain procedures.

1. Determine if a violation has in effect occurred. Never accuse or report alleged instances to a higher authority without verification.
2. If an instance is verified, tactfully inform the violator of the specific criteria to use so that future violations can be avoided. Presented properly, the information will be accepted as constructive.
3. If advice is unheeded and further infractions occur, bring them to the attention of the teacher's supervisor - a team leader or department chair - who can handle the matter as an evaluation procedure.
4. Inform the person who has reported the alleged violation of the procedures being used.

Skill 2.5 **Demonstrating knowledge of issues related to the effective use of current, relevant information processes and resources (e.g., bibliographies, promotional materials, online tutorials, Web site designs), including emerging technologies**

Technology has changed the instructional resources now available to schools. There are wide arrays of resources that can be found in multiple formats. Types of resources that are used in schools can include:

- **Overhead transparencies** are still a viable tool for instruction. Transparencies are easily created using computer software and films meant for either inkjet or laser printers.
- **Multimedia Presentations** can accentuate material being presented to students. While the technology has become more readily available, availability of equipment can often be an issue. However, the format is often more appealing than transparencies.
- **Audio recordings** are also widely available. Older formats such as vinyl records have been replaced by cassette tapes and CDs. Podcasts or audio files are popular formats. Podcasting is a method of publishing files through subscriptions that are available to users. These recordings can be played directly from the computer or downloaded onto various devices.
- **Video recordings** have taken over the role of filmstrips and slideshows. Video is more animated than its predecessor and can be found in various formats such as video tape, DVDs, Blue Ray discs and video streamed from online sources.
- **Print material** is still prevalent in libraries. Books can also be found in audio format as well as electronic formats called ebooks.
- **Computer Software** stored on CD-ROMS also supports many learning opportunities. Schools physically store the software on either a single machine or on a server for the sharing of the software across the school's network. Special licenses are required for network use.
- **Online Programs** have taken over the role of resources once housed within the walls of the media center. Some resources are subscription based but are still considerably cheaper than upgrading software on CD-ROMs. One downfall of this format can be the space it takes up on the district's bandwidth. Online resources containing a great deal of video can cause a network to perform considerably slower.

Specific uses for technology related items include:

- **Computerized databases** like online dictionaries, encyclopedias and information databases can be easily accessed. These databases are easily searched using keywords and generally contain cross-references to similar information. The speed of computerized databases dramatically reduces time searching for information.
- **Online catalogs** include catalogs of information similar to a database or catalogs for ordering resources. The information can be located using keyword searches that allow the user to drill down for more information.
- **CD-ROMs** are compact discs that contain software and other multi-media resources. The resources can include electronic atlases, encyclopedias, and simulations. Like the online encyclopedias, the storage capacity of CDs allows for relevant video and audio to be included with the articles. Interactive resources such as simulations can also be incorporated in these resources.
- **Video** can be found in a wide variety of formats. Videotapes in various formats are still part of the resources found in many school library media centers. Upgrading equipment and formats can be costly, so school budgets may still require use of older formats such as VHS. Many video cameras used in schools utilize smaller types of tapes such as Hi 8 or Mini DVD cassettes for recording. Video can also be found on DVDs. As technology changes and the format for videos improve, schools will eventually move to newer formats as they arise.

When equipment and formats become an issue, schools can turn to online videos to supplement their collection. A variety of educational videos can be found online. Companies such as United Streaming focus on providing quality educational videos. The main issue with viewing videos online is the bandwidth these resources require. Bandwidth is the amount of information that can be sent over a network. When a file such as a video takes up a large part of the bandwidth, other resources begin to slow down. There are various formats of video, and some require more space than others.

Video file extensions can include:
.avi – Audio Video Interactive file
.mpeg – MPEG Video Files
.rm – Real Media File
.qt – QuickTime Movie
.wmv – Windows Media Video File

Because of bandwidth concerns, careful consideration and consultation with the network administrator needs to take place before the use of viewing videos online becomes widespread.

- **Audio** can also be found in a variety of formats within schools. The issue for using older formats involves the cost to upgrade equipment. Cassette tapes contain both music and audio versions of books. As cassettes become worn or damaged they are being replaced by CDs. Audio clips can be found online, and these are often called podcasts. Podcasts are audio files found online, many of which are in the format of a radio broadcast. As with video, the use of streaming audio from the Internet does cut into a network's bandwidth. However, audio files are not usually as large.

TEACHER CERTIFICATION STUDY GUIDE

COMPETENCY 3.0 UNDERSTAND CHARACTERISTICS OF LITERATURE FOR CHILDREN AND YOUNG ADULTS AND STRATEGIES FOR PROMOTING LITERACY

Skill 3.1 Demonstrating knowledge of historical and contemporary trends and multicultural issues in reading material for children and young adults

During the last 50 years, literature for children and adolescents has grown to thousands of new titles per year. Many of these new titles follow trends, as the authors and publishers are very aware of the market and the social changes affecting their products. Books are selected for libraries because of their social, psychological and intellectual value. Collections must also contain materials that recognize needs for exposure to diverse cultures and ethnicities. Because there are so many popular titles in the young adult area that deal with controversial subjects, school library media specialists are faced with juggling the preferences of their student patrons with the need to provide worthwhile literature and maintain intellectual freedom in the face of increasing censorship. For instance, books such as Robert Cormier's *Chocolate War*, *Return to Chocolate War,* and *Fade* deal with the darker side of teen life. Paul Zindel's *Pigman* and *The Undertaker's Gone Bananas* deal with the stresses in teen life with a touch of humor. Both of these authors provide important material to the emotional development of teenagers, and examples such as these should not be omitted from a collection because they portray negative aspects of developing adolescents.

Books for younger children generally include picture books. Notable illustrators of children's books include Marcia Brown, Leo and Diane Dillon, Barbara Dooney, Nonny Hogrogian, David Macaulay, Emily Arnold McCully, Allen Say, Maurice Sendak, Chris Van Allsburg and David Wiesner.

Books for young readers teach them about relationships to the world around them and to other people and things in that world. These topics help them learn how things operate and how to overcome fears. Like the still popular fairy tales of previous centuries, some of today's popular children's books are fantasies or allegories, such as Robert O'Brien's *Mrs. Frisby and the Rats of NIMH.*

Popular books for preadolescents deal more with establishing relationships with members of the opposite sex (e.g., Sweet Valley High series) and learning to cope with their changing bodies, personalities or life situations, as displayed in Judy Blume's *Are You There, God? It's Me, Margaret*. Adolescents are still interested in the fantasy and science fiction genres as well as the popular juvenile fiction. Middle school students still read the *Little House on the Prairie* series and the mysteries of the Hardy Boys and Nancy Drew. Teens value the works of Emily and Charlotte Brontë, Willa Cather, Jack London, William Shakespeare and Mark Twain as much as those of Piers Anthony, S.E. Hinton, Madeleine L'Engle, Stephen King and J.R.R. Tolkien. Despite their publication dates, most children are still enthralled in the classics of English literature.

Popular genres and their notable authors in children's literature include:

- **Fantasy** focuses on the supernatural or incorporates magic. Famous fantasy writer for young adults include: Piers Anthony, Ursula LeGuin and Ann McCaffrey
- **Horror** details scary or horrific stories that may focus on monsters, paranormal events and the spirit world. Popular horror writers include: V.C. Andrews and Stephen King
- **Juvenile fiction** focuses on stories based upon imagination, not on fact. Popular writers for this genre include: Judy Blume, Robert Cormier, Rosa Guy, Virginia Hamilton, S.E. Hinton, M.E. Kerr, Harry Mazer, Norma Fox Mazer, Richard Newton Peck, Cynthia Voight and Paul Zindel.
- **Science fiction** focuses on imaginary stories based on technology or science. These stories are often based on the future and can include beings from another planet and time travel. Popular authors include: Isaac Asimov, Ray Bradbury, Arthur Clarke, Frank Herbert, Larry Niven and H.G. Wells.
- **Folk Tales** are stories that have been passed down through generations by word of mouth.
- **Historical Fiction** is centered on fictional characters that are placed in the midst of some historical event.
- **Picture books** (and illustrated story books) are most often works of fiction that are colorfully illustrated. Notable illustrators of children's books include: Marcia Brown, Leo and Diane Dillon, Barbara Dooney, Nonny Hogrogian, David Macaulay, Emily Arnold McCully, Allen Say, Maurice Sendak, Chris Van Allsburg and David Wiesner.

Book awards are another source for lists of quality literature. Two of the most widely recognized awards are the Caldecott and Newberry Awards.
Each year an outstanding illustrator of a children's book is honored for his or her outstanding work by being presented with the Caldecott Medal. This award was created in honor of Randolph Caldecott and is distributed annually by the *Association for Library Service for Children*. It was first presented in 1938.

Award winners for the past fifteen years include:

- 2007 – **Flotsam** by David Wiesner
- 2006 - **The Hello, Goodbye Window** illustrated by Chris Raschka and written by Norton Juster
- 2005 - **Kitten's First Full Moon** by Kevin Henkes
- 2004 - **The Man Who Walked Between the Towers** by Mordicai Gerstein
- 2003 - **My Friend Rabbit** by Eric Rohmann
- 2002 - **The Three Pigs** by David Wiesner
- 2001 - **So You Want to Be President?** illustrated by David Small and written by Judith St. George
- 2000 - **Had a Little Overcoat** by Simms Taback
- 1999 - **Snowflake Bentley** illustrated by Mary Azarian and written by Jacqueline Briggs Martin
- 1998 – **Rapunzel** by Paul O. Zelinsky
- 1997 – **Golem** by David Wisniewski
- 1996 - **Officer Buckle and Gloria** by Peggy Rathmann
- 1995 - **Smoky Night** illustrated by David Diaz; text: Eve Bunting
- 1994 - **Grandfather's Journey** by Allen Say and edited by Walter Lorraine
- 1993 - **Mirette on the High Wire** by Emily Arnold McCully

Notable illustrators of children's books include Marcia Brown, Leo and Diane Dillon, Barbara Dooney, Nonny Hogrogian, David Macaulay, Emily Arnold McCully, Allen Say, Maurice Sendak, Chris Van Allsburg and David Wiesner.

Bookseller John Newbery was the first to publish literature for children on any scale in the second half of 18th century England, the great outpouring of children's literature came 100 years later in the Victorian Age. Novels such as Charles Dickens' *Oliver Twist*, Robert Louis Stevenson's *Treasure Island*, and Rudyard Kipling's *Jungle Book*, have become classics in children's literature, even though they were not solely written for children. These books not only helped children understand the world they lived in, but the books also satisfied their interest in adventure.

The Newberry Award was created in 1992 to honor John Newberry. This award is presented to an author of the most notable work of fiction for children or young adults.

Newberry awarded books for the past fifteen years include:

> 2007 - *The Higher Power of Lucky* written by Susan Patron **and** illustrated by Matt Phelan
> 2006 - *Criss Cross* by Lynne Rae Perkins
> 2005 - *Kira-Kira* by Cynthia Kadohata
> 2004 - *The Tale of Despereaux: Being the Story of a Mouse, a Princess, Some Soup, and a Spool of Thread* by Kate DiCamillo and illustrated by Timothy Basil Ering
> 2003 - *Crispin: The Cross of Lead* by Avi
> 2002 - *A Single Shard* by Linda Sue Park
> 2001 - *A Year Down Yonder* by Richard Peck
> 2000 - *Bud, Not Buddy* by Christopher Paul Curtis
> 1999 - *Holes* by Louis Sachar
> 1998 - *Out of the Dust* by Karen Hesse
> 1997 - *The View from Saturday* **by E.L. Konigsburg**
> 1996 - *The Midwife's Apprentice* by Karen Cushman
> 1995 - *Walk Two Moons* by Sharon Creech
> 1994 - *The Giver* by Lois Lowry

Two of the many other awards that have come about in recent years include The Coretta Scott King Award and the Laura Ingalls Wilder Award. The Coretta Scott King Award is presented to outstanding African Americans authors and illustrators for their outstanding educational contributions. The Laura Ingalls Wilder award honors an author or illustrator who published books in the United States that have made a significant and lasting contribution to literature for children.

At the state level, Georgia presents the Georgia Book Award to the best picture book and the best middle grade novel. A group of teachers and media specialists select 20 nominees from a list of books. During the school year teachers and media specialists in participating schools share these books with students. Students then vote for their favorites in the specific category.

Past winners in the picture book category include:

> 2005-06 - *My Lucky Day* by Kieko Kasza
> 2004-05 - *Stanley's Party* by Linda Bailey and Bill Slavin
> 2003-04 - *Hooway for Wodney Wat* by Helen Lester and Lynn Munsinger
> 2002-03 - *Stand Tall Molly Lou Melon* by Patty Lovell and David Catrow
> 2001-02 - *Bark, George* by Jules Feiffer
> 2000-01 - *Verdi* by Janell Cannon
> 1999-2000 - *No, David* by David Shannon

Past middle grade winners include:

    2005-06 – ***Runt*** by Marion Dane Bauer
    2004-05 - ***Loser*** by Jerry Spinelli
    2003-04 - ***Skeleton Man*** by Joseph Bruchac
    2002-03 - ***The Power of Un*** by Nancy Etchemendy
    2001-02 - ***Danger in the Desert*** by T. S. Fields
    2000-01 - ***My Life as a Fifth Grade Comedian*** by Elizabeth Levy
    1999-2000 - ***The Imp That Ate My Homework*** by Laurence Yep
    1998-99 - ***Frindle*** by Andrew Clements

Skill 3.2   Demonstrating knowledge of strategies for collaborating with teachers to integrate literature into the curriculum

One of the single most important parts of a successful school library media program is collaboration between the school library media specialist and classroom teachers. To support the collaborative process there are key skills the media specialist must possess. These include:

- Flexibility – have the ability to adjust to the differing needs of staff and students. Be flexible with times and scheduling.
- Curriculum Expert – get to know the curriculum being taught at the grade levels being served. This makes the media specialist and invaluable partner in developing and enhancing the curriculum.
- Leadership – set the path in which the media program should move towards. Set goals and expectations for the media program. Be an advocate for the teachers as well.
- Approachability – establish good rapport with staff and students as someone they know who is willing to go above and beyond.
- Persistence - keep the media program moving forward.

As a library media specialist works collaboratively with the classroom teacher the specialist's main focus is to create lessons and activities that integrate information skills into the curriculum. Achievement of the design of collaborative teaching units with supplemental or total involvement of the library media center resources and services satisfy levels 9 and 10 of Loertscher's eleven level taxonomy. The taxonomy assumes the active involvement of the school library media specialist in the total school program.

One key resource in the collaboration process is the Media Committee, often known as the Media Advisory Committee (MAC) or Media / Technology Advisory Committee (MTAC). The role of the Media Committee is to work collaboratively with the media specialist to determine program direction, make budgeting and purchasing decisions, and provide feedback on all topics relating to the media center. The media committee is a good place to begin a collaborative relationship with teachers.

Developing lifelong readers plays an important role in the library media program. The library media specialists work closely with the teacher to teach students how to locate and use information. They also work to develop a love for literature through literature enrichment activities like book talks and reading promotions. Individual learning styles based on theories such as Howard Gardner's Multiple Intelligences are taken into consideration and they work.

Skill 3.3 **Demonstrating knowledge of issues related to the selection and recommendation of literature for a school library media program (e.g., age-appropriateness, cultural diversity, developmental levels, format diversity)**

Helping students find literature that meets their needs developmentally is essential to improving their learning.

Students in preschool and kindergarten need literature that they will find enjoyable and that helps them to become familiar with language patterns. The story needs to be easy for these readers to follow. Books that are to be read independently should have plenty of picture support, and books that are to be read aloud to students need to be engaging and provide opportunities for students to interact with the text.

Students in grades 1 and 2 are developing literacy skills. They begin constructing meaning and building their site word vocabulary. As independent readers these students need books that utilize various cueing systems such as syntax, semantics and the use of picture support. These students are beginning to see themselves as readers.

3rd and 4th graders should have acquired basic reading skills and are working to build fluency. They are beginning to read longer stories with fewer pictures. Students at this age are also beginning to use textbooks as a source for information and must begin to read for deeper meaning as well as for enjoyment.

Beyond the elementary grades, students will read for a variety of reasons. They are most likely fluent readers. When reading for pleasure, students should be encouraged to select books based on their interest. These students are also expected to read for information in either textbooks or from other information resources.

In addition to developing language skills and an interest in reading, the school library is a powerful place to increase cultural awareness among students. The American Library Association strongly advocates the use of the school library media program to address and celebrate the diverse populations within a school.

Here are simple ways a media program can address this topic:

- Provide resources that address a variety of cultures. This should include both fiction and non-fiction works.
- Plan celebrations that focus upon various cultures or student populations.
- Invite guest speakers related to these topics.

Skill 3.4 Demonstrating knowledge of how to use literacy research to select literature that facilitates the reading process and develops fluency in readers

When selecting resources for a school library it is important to work in collaboration with teachers and follow district and state selection policies. Find the resources can be a daunting task because there are many sources of information.

The best places to begin are review publications such as:

- *School Library Journal*
- *Booklist*
- *The Horn Book*
- *Wilson Book Review*

Each of these provides concise reviews on current books. *The Horn Book* is a collective guide that will list the ratings from the other sources listed.

The International Reading Association (IRA) is a great resource for locating research on literacy research and standards for reading. Their web site provides information such as:

- Recommended reading lists both for student and professional use
- Online resources
- Videos
- Links to research
- Information pertaining to literacy for all ages.

Other places to locate resources include:

1. Companies who offer collection lists designed for elementary, middle, secondary, or special content schools, such as the vocational or performing arts. These lists are used most often for opening a new school library media center. School library media specialists and review committees customize these lists to user needs.
2. Publisher's catalogs. These are good starting points for locating specific titles and comparison shopping.
3. Vendors representing one or more publishers. Too little has been said about establishing good relationships with vendors who have access to demonstration materials and can make them available for review. Naturally, they want to sell their employers' products; however, most are familiar with their competitors' product lines and work collaboratively to help schools secure the most appropriate materials.
4. Bibliographic indexes of subject specific titles with summaries. These indexes are not free and are most cost effective if housed in the district professional library. The same is true of *Books in Print*, in print and non-print formats. Because its contents change significantly from year to year, many districts cannot justify its cost, relying instead on direct communication with publishers to determine a book's status.
5. Publications such as *Publisher's Weekly* provide information on the latest releases, current topics and book reviews.

Another source of providing a wide variety of literature is to include books that have been noted by organizations that specialize in reading. Each year the American Library Association, Children's Book Council and International Reading Association publish lists of notable books for children.

Skill 3.5 Identifying strategies for developing a sense of appreciation for literature in others and for promoting the habit of lifelong reading

By developing an appreciation for literature, students begin to develop lifelong reading skills. There are steps that can be taken by the media specialist as well as the classroom teacher to build a greater appreciation for literature. These can include:
- Teaching students about different genres. Presenting a unit on poetry, folk tales, fairy tales, fiction or non-fiction.
- Conduct author studies.
- Have student create literature response products.
- Develop a repertoire of reading strategies to build fluency. These could include using context clues, chunking, etc.
- Teach students to identify parts of a story such as plot and conclusion.

The more students understand the construction of literature, the better they begin to understand and connect with the information they read. The more connections they make with literature, the stronger the habit of reading will become.

COMPETENCY 4.0 UNDERSTAND STRATEGIES FOR PROVIDING ACCESS TO INFORMATION, IDEAS AND LITERATURE.

Skill 4.1 Identifying relationships among facilities, programs and environment that affect student learning

Because of the diversity of services provided in a modern school library media center, it is important to foster a user-friendly atmosphere, one in which the patron is not only welcomed as a user of resources but is also involved as a producer of ideas and materials.

Considering the academic and personal needs of the user, the library media program should provide an atmosphere in which users can attain both basic skills and enrichment goals.

Factors that influence the atmosphere:

1. Proximity to academic classes.
2. Aesthetic appearance.
3. Acoustical ceilings and floor coverings.
4. Adequate temperature control.
5. Adequate, non-glare lighting with controls for different types of viewing activities.
6. Comfortable, appropriately sized, and durable furnishings.
7. Diverse, plentiful, and current resources that are attractive to handle as well as easy to use.
8. Courteous, helpful personnel, using supervisory techniques that encourage self-exploration and creativity while protecting the rules of library etiquette.

Skill 4.2 Demonstrating knowledge of practices that support flexible, open access for the library media center resources and services for classes, small groups and individuals

The issue of flexible access is especially distressing to elementary school library media specialists who are placed in the "related arts wheel," providing planning time for art, music and physical education teachers. "Closed" or rigid scheduling (i.e., scheduling classes to meet regularly for instruction in the library) prohibits the implementation of the integrated program philosophy essential to the principles of intellectual freedom.

The AASL Position Statement on Flexible Scheduling asserts that schools must adopt a philosophy of full integration of library media into the total educational program. This integration assures a partnership among students, teachers and school library media specialists in the use of readily accessible materials and services when they are appropriate to the classroom curriculum

All parties in the school community - teachers, principal, district administration, and school board - must share the responsibility for contributing to flexible access.

Research on the validity of flexible access reinforces the need for cooperative planning with teachers, an objective that cannot be met if the school library media specialist has no time for the required planning sessions. Rigid scheduling denies students the freedom to come to the library during the school day for pleasurable reading and self-motivated inquiry activities vital to the development of critical thinking, problem solving and exploratory skills. Without flexible access, the library becomes just another self-contained classroom.

Skill 4.3   Recognizing factors involved in the physical design and furnishing of a flexible, functional and barrier-free library media center (e.g., access to technology, accommodations for learners with physical disabilities or other special needs)

The specifics of spatial arrangement depend upon the types and quantities of resources and services provided. New school design should place the media center in a central location that is easily accessible to all academic areas. Within the center itself the following spatial arrangement factors should be addressed.

1. A large central area for reading, listening, viewing and computing, which has ready access to materials and equipment. AASL/AECT guidelines recommend that this main seating area be 25% - 75% of the total square footage allocation, depending on program requirements. 40 square feet should be allotted per student user. Within this area or peripheral to it, there should be smaller areas that provide for independent study or accommodate students with physical impairments. Seating should be adequate to accommodate the number of users during peak hours. SAC guidelines recommend floor space and seating to accommodate 10% of the student body, but the media center should not be expected to seat fewer than 40 or more than 100 students at one time.
2. Areas for small or medium-sized group activities. These areas may be acoustically special spaces adjacent to the central seating area or conference rooms, computer labs or storytelling space. AASL/AECT recommends 1 - 3 areas or approximately 150 square feet with ample electrical outlets, good lighting and acoustics, and a wall screen.

3. Space to house and display the collection. Materials that can be circulated outside the center should be easily accessible from the main seating area. Index tools should be highly visible and in the immediate proximity to the collections they index. A supervised circulation desk with easy access to non-circulable databases (i.e., periodicals, CD- ROM disks, microform and videotape collections) should be close to the center's main entrance. AASL/AECT recommends a minimum of 400 square feet for stacks with an additional 200 foot allowance per 500 additional students.
4. A reference materials area within or adjacent to the central seating area. The recommended area allowance is part of the total allotted for the stacks.
5. Space for a professional collection and work area where the faculty and media professionals can work privately. This area should be approximately 1 square foot per student.
6. Administrative offices, with areas for resource and equipment processing, materials duplication and business materials storage. An area no smaller than 200 square feet should be available for offices alone and double that area if in-house processing is done.
7. Equipment storage and circulation area close to administrative offices and with access to outside corridor. Space for maintenance and repair is optional depending on available staff to attend to these duties. This space should be no less than 400 square feet for storage with another 150 square feet if repair facilities are necessary.
8. A media production area with space and equipment for production of audio and videotaping, graphics design, photography, computer programming and photocopying. (In some secondary schools, a dark room is included. Other schools with commercial photography classes and a full photography lab may seek services through the photography teacher.) This area may be as small as 50 square feet or as large as 700 square feet in a school with 500 students depending on the amount of equipment required to suit media production needs; in a school with 1000 or more students, at least 700-900 square feet should be allotted for media production.
9. A television production studio for formal TV production class instruction and preparing special programming. Space for distribution of closed circuit programs and satellite transmissions should also be provided. A 1600 square foot studio (preferably 40' x 40' x 15') should be available whenever television classes are taught or studio videotaping is a program priority. AASL/AECT guidelines allow alternatives, namely for studio space available at the district for the use of students or mini-studios/portable videotape units where videotaping is done on a small scale.
10. A large multi-purpose room adjacent to the media center is recommended, but optional in many schools. AASL/AECT recommends that this room be 700-900 square feet (i.e., classroom size) in a school with 500 students or 900-1200 square feet in a school with 1000 students. This room should be equipped for making all types of media presentations.

11. A network / server head-end area that would house network services, telephone equipment and video distribution equipment for the entire building. The space should be from 450- 800 square feet. Equipment for this room may include network server, routers switches, telephone patch panel, cabling and wireless devices.
12. Network access and power outlets should be available throughout the entire media center to accommodate circulation search stations, student work stations and other electronic devices.

Because of the diversity of services provided in a modern school library media center, these spatial requirements help to foster a user-friendly atmosphere, one in which the patron is not only welcomed as a user of resources but is also given the space to collaborate on ideas and materials.

All facilities must provide access to those with physical handicaps. A few of the recommendations are:

1. Work surfaces at least 30" from the floor.
2. Clear aisle width for wheelchair access.
3. Large, clearly visible signs that include accommodations for the visually impaired.
4. Devices for the visually and hearing impaired. One such device is the Kurzweil reader for the visually impaired. This device reads aloud scanned or electronic text.

The library media program, in considering the academic and personal needs of the user, should provide an atmosphere in which users can attain both basic skills and enrichment goals.

Factors that influence the atmosphere:

1. Proximity to academic classes.
2. Aesthetic appearance.
3. Acoustical ceilings and floor coverings.
4. Adequate temperature control
5. Adequate, non-glare lighting with controls for different types of viewing activities.
6. Comfortable, appropriately sized and durable furnishings.
7. Diverse, plentiful and current resources that are attractive to handle as well as easy to use.
8. Courteous, helpful personnel, using supervisory techniques that encourage self-exploration and creativity while protecting the rules of library etiquette.

Whether remodeling an existing media center or building a new one, it is important to take into consideration the American Disabilities Act regulations. Key documents include:

- ADA Accessibility Guidelines for Buildings and Facilities (ADAAG)
- Americans with Disabilities Act
- Telecommunications Act of 1996 (Section 255)

These documents outline the guidelines for furniture height, aisle width (42 inches), and aisle space around the circulation desk and card catalog.

Skill 4.4　Demonstrating knowledge of elements of design to consider in promoting efficient and appropriate use of the library media center (e.g., traffic patterns, work flow, patron use)

The school level planning committee should be comprised of the school library media specialist, the technology specialist, the principal, teachers, students, parents, a school board member, the system-level media director, the system level technology director, and the superintendent. The responsibilities of this group are to assist with the planning process, determine education specifications, determine technology needs, select furniture, and set priorities for the essentials needed to ensure the success of the school library media program.

There are important design elements to consider when renovating or building new facilities.

1. Traffic flow should provide easy, logical access to all spaces.
2. A realistic assessment of security needs will provide for material detection systems, alarms or locks to protect electronic equipment, and convenient placement of communications devices.
3. Proper placement of electrical outlets, fire extinguishers, smoke detectors and thermostats ensures safety for users and convenience for the staff.
4. Provision must be made for the physically impaired to have barrier-free access to the center and its resources.
5. All areas requiring supervision should be readily visible from other areas of the center.
6. There should be a carefully planned relationship among spaces used for supporting activities and services.

Skill 4.5 Demonstrating knowledge of collaborative techniques for creating and maintaining an attractive, positive climate in a technologically rich, student-centered library media center

Collaboration is the key when designing learning opportunities for students. By working together the media specialist and the classroom teacher can design integrated lessons that focus on information literacy, the use of technology and appreciation of literature.

In this regard, the school library media specialist should strive to provide reading programs throughout the year that are based upon the recommendations from state agencies. These activities could include family events, book talks, special guests and the use of various online resources.

When focusing on the integration of information technology it is important to consult the technology requirements for each grade level and to assure that these requirements are in line with the needs and requests of teachers.

Attention should also be given to the availability of resources for students beyond the school day in order for students to complete work assignment by their classroom teacher. This could include extended hours of operation and home access to school supported web resources.

Skill 4.6 Identifying methods for using research-based data, including action research, to improve the library media program

It is important to note that evaluation is an ongoing process. It must occur prior to determining goals and objectives and on a regular basis thereafter to ensure they are being met.

A wide variety of evaluation criteria may be used. The criteria may be:

1. Diagnostic. These are standards based on conditions existing in programs that have already been judged as excellent.
2. Projective. These standards are guidelines for conditions as they ought to be.
3. Quantitative. These standards require numerical measurement.
4. Qualitative. These standards are designed to express essentially the measured criteria as quantitative without exact numerical amounts. Action research is a form of qualitative data collection that occurs when educators reflect upon their teaching by observing occurrences in a school or classroom and identifying problems. The educator then devises steps or actions to correct the problem.

Most school library media program evaluations have been diagnostic or qualitative. Diagnostic prescriptions alone make no allowances for specific conditions in given schools and are often interpreted too liberally; in addition, qualitative prescriptions alone are difficult to measure or sustain. Projective standards are usually broad national guidelines which are best used as long-range goals. Preferably, a program evaluation utilizing a combination of quantitative and qualitative standards produces results that can lead to modified objectives. Statistics to substantiate quantitative standards can be derived from:

1. Usage statistics from automated circulation systems. These indicate frequency of materials use.
2. Inventory figures. Resource turnover, loss and damage, and missing materials statistics indicate extent of use. Total materials count can substantiate materials per student criteria.
3. Individual circulation logs. Such logs indicate the frequency of patron use of library materials and the types of materials used.
4. Class scheduling log. Depending on the amount of data acquired when a visit is scheduled, several facts can be determined: proportion of staff and student body using materials and services; the frequency of use of specific resources or services; the age levels of users; specific subgroups being served; and subject matter preferences.

Evidence of meeting qualitative standards can be derived from:

1. **Lesson plans.** Careful planning will reveal the frequency of use of resources and specific classroom objectives planned cooperatively with faculty. The plan should also specify the effectiveness with which the students achieved the lesson objectives.
2. **Personnel evaluations.** Most districts have either formative evaluations, summative evaluations, or both for professional, para-professional, or non-professional staff. Student aides should receive educational credit for their services hours. Completion of specific skills and termination grades can provide both quantitative and qualitative data.
3. **Surveys.** A systematic written evaluation should be conducted annually to obtain input from students, teachers and parents on the success of program objectives.
4. **Conferences / Library Advisory Committee meetings.** Comments from faculty members and students can provide qualitative assessment of the value of the materials and services provided.
5. **Criterion-referenced or teacher made tests**. These assessments can be used to evaluate student effectiveness in acquiring information skills or content area skills.

Once an initial program evaluation has been completed, program goals and objectives may be determined. These goals and objectives help to break down the overall vision for school library media program into areas that the school feels are most important for its successful operation. Some of these goals may already be determined by national or state guidelines that a district's administrators have agreed to maintain. Sometimes, a district operates without a program to guide school library media centers. In that case each school must be responsible not only for setting its own criteria but also for inspiring some district planning.

The first step would be to define major goals (i.e., a long range plan). A goal is a broad statement of an intended outcome that reflects the mission of the school library media program that provides direction. Therefore, when planning a school library media program based on an assessment of school and student characteristics, the program planning team should factor in these elements.

A long-range plan should:

1. Extend from 3-5 years.
2. Incorporate the goals of the other departments (e.g., grade levels or content teams) in the school.
3. Be stated in terms that are non-limiting. The goal should be an achievable aim, not a pipe dream.

Specific goals for school library media centers are outlined in *Information Power: Building Partnerships for Learning.* Key points include:

- providing access to resources and information through integrated activities on a variety of levels,
- providing physical access to a wide variety of resources and information from various locations including outside agencies and electronic resources,
- assisting patrons in locating and evaluating information,
- collaborating with teachers and others,
- facilitating the lifelong learning process,
- building a school library media program that acts as the hub for all learning within the school,
- providing resources that embrace cultural and social differences and support concepts of intellectual freedom

After the major goals have been defined, objectives must be determined. An objective is a specific statement of a measurable result that will occur by a particular time (i.e., it must specify the conditions and criteria to be met effectively.) Objectives reflect short- term priorities, and they must have a specific format. Objectives must contain an action verb and must be measurable.

A few of the action verbs often seen in objectives are: discuss, define, compare, identify, explain and design.

A short-range plan should be one part of a longer range plan that is:

1. Accomplishable in one year or less.
2. Linked meaningfully in a logical progression to the expressed goal.
3. Flexible, as most objectives must be processed through affected groups before finalization.

Using an Olympic athlete as an example, an appropriate set of goals and objectives might go as follows:

Goal: To win an Olympic Medal.

Objectives:

1. To increase my speed by .05 seconds per meter by June 30.
2. To double my practice time during the two weeks before the competition begins.
3. To lose 3 lbs. before my weigh-in.

If translated into goals and objectives for library media centers, the set may read as the following:

Goal: To develop a collection more suited to the academic demands of the curriculum

Objectives:

1. To increase non-fiction collection by 10% in the next school year.
2. To ensure readability levels suited to gifted students for 5% of new selections.

Goal: To provide telecommunications services within three years.

Objectives:

1. To design a model for instructional use in 1996.
2. To plan for equipment and facilities needs in 1997.
3. To implement the model with a control group in 1998.

If a school seeks or wishes to maintain accreditation with the Southern Association of Colleges and Schools (SAC), using that organization's recommendations is an excellent way to set program goals and objectives. Because SAC requires every accredited school to conduct an intensive ten year reevaluation and a five year interim review, the library media center program planners may wish to coordinate their own study with SAC's reviews.

Skill 4.7   Recognizing organizational structures that enhance or impede physical or intellectual access to ideas and information

It is the goal of a library to provide access to resources covering a wide range of topics, cultural differences and viewpoints. There are many organizations that fight to preserve the First Amendment in the nation's libraries.

One of the strongest allies to libraries is the American Library Association (ALA). They provide overall guidelines for libraries in their quest for preserving intellectual freedom.

School libraries have an additional resource through the American Association of School Libraries. This ALA affiliate advocates excellence and the development of school libraries.

In regards to general First Amendment issues, American Civil Liberties Union (ACLU) has the mission of preserving the freedom of speech for all Americans.

The Freedom to Read Foundation also focuses on freedom of speech as well as the right of an individual to read and listen to the ideas of others.

There are also entities that work to restrict access to certain materials as a way of protecting others, generally children, from what they deem to be objectionable content. The problem occurs when the viewpoints these entities wish to restrict aren't necessarily offensive to another group.

Local groups such as school boards and other elected officials receive pressure from parents to remove or restrict materials.

The Children's Internet Protection Act (CIPA) is designed to protect children from objectionable Internet content. In this act, schools that receive some form of E-rate funding must have an Internet filter in place to protect students from objectionable content such as pornography. Filters aren't foolproof and there are always things that slip through. Also, the filters often get tweaked to go beyond the original theory behind the act and begin to block other items that teachers or administrators don't want students to view. Such filters cause debates over the grey areas that occur in potentially objectionable content.

| SUBAREA II. | INFORMATION LITERACY SKILLS |

COMPETENCY 5.0   UNDERSTAND INFORMATION RESOURCES AND STRATEGIES FOR LOCATING AND ACCESSING INFORMATION RESOURCES FOR A PARTICULAR PURPOSE.

Skill 5.1   Identifying types, characteristics and uses of various print, nonprint and electronic information resources (e.g., encyclopedias, dictionaries, online services, periodicals)

Most libraries contain print resources that fall either into the reference category or that of circulating materials.

Reference materials are generally housed in a special location within the media center. These materials are for patrons to use, but they are rarely allowed to be checked out and taken home. Reference materials include: almanacs, dictionaries, encyclopedias, special sets of books, atlases and manuals.

Circulating materials are those books that can be checked out. They cover a wide range of topics and can include works of non-fiction as well as fiction.

With the flood of technological advances in the past few decades, school library media centers have a wealth of non-print information available. Examples include:

- **Computerized databases** where items like online dictionaries, encyclopedias and direct databases of information can be easily accessed. These databases are easily searched using keywords and generally contain cross-references to similar information. The speed of computerized databases dramatically reduces time searching for information.

- **Online catalogs** may refer to catalogs of information similar to a database or catalogs for ordering resources. The information can be located using keyword searches that allow the user to drill down for more information.

- **CD-ROMs** contain software and other multimedia resources that include include electronic atlases, encyclopedias and simulations, among other materials. Like the online encyclopedias, the storage capacity of CDs allows for relevant video and audio to be included with the articles. Interactive resources such as simulations can also be incorporated in these resources.

- **Video** can be found in a wide variety of formats. Videotapes in various formats are still a part of the resources found in many school library media centers. Upgrading equipment and formats can be costly, so school budgets may still require older formats such as VHS be used. Many video cameras used in schools utilize smaller types of tapes such as Hi 8 or Mini DVD cassettes for recording. Video can also be found on DVDs. As technology changes and the format for videos improve, schools will eventually move to newer formats as they arise.

  When equipment and formats become an issue, schools can turn to online videos to supplement their collection. A variety of educational videos can be found online. Companies such as United Streaming focus on providing quality educational videos. The main issue with viewing videos online is the bandwidth these resources require. Bandwidth is the amount of information that can be sent over a network. When a file such as a video takes up a large part of the bandwidth other resources begin to slow down. Careful consideration and consultation with the network administrator needs to take place before the use of viewing videos online becomes widespread.

- **Audio** can also be found in a variety of formats within schools. The issue for using older formats involves the cost to upgrade equipment. Cassette tapes contain both music and audio versions of books. As cassettes become worn or damaged they are being replaced by CDs. Audio clips can be found online, and these are often called podcasts. Podcasts are audio files found online, many of which are in the format of a radio broadcast. As with video, the use of streaming audio from the Internet does cut into a network's bandwidth. However, audio files are not usually as large.

Skill 5.2 Recognizing and comparing the advantages and limitations of various information resources, formats and services

In comparing various types of information formats, each has their strengths and weaknesses.

- Print resources are very important for young learners because they need to touch and feel a book as they learn how to use it. However, if a reader is searching for information, books can be more cumbersome and require more time to find information.

- Computerized resources are generally easy to search and locate information. The interactivity of such information can provide more in depth understanding than what could be gained by only reading the material. One disadvantage is that some students find it difficult to read large articles on the computer and will often opt to print the articles instead of reading them online.

- Video can be found in a variety of formats. The use of video as a teaching tool is necessary to the success of visual learners. Schools must have the equipment to play each type of video used. Online video streams can drastically reduce the speed at which a network operates. The use of online video in conjunction with other network applications needs to be closely monitored to keep the network from becoming severely hampered.

- As with video, schools need to maintain the equipment needed to play the types of audio available. Online audio streams can be quite informative, but do need to be carefully monitored. Audio formats are not as interactive as some other formats, but are a very effective learning tool for auditory learners.

Skill 5.3   Demonstrating knowledge of strategies for locating specific information in various types of resources (e.g., indices, electronic databases, catalogs) and applying criteria for selecting an appropriate resource for locating specific information

Utilizing information retrieval systems is very similar to searching for information in other formats. The user may need to know specific keywords, Boolean operators or even wild cards.

Depending upon the system, the researcher may need to know specific details surrounding the database itself. They may need to know key database field names or categories to define their search. For example, if the school nurse needs to find health information regarding a particular student, the nurse would need to know how the name categories are arranged. If the database searches for the first and last name together the nurse may have difficulty locating the student if he or she only types in the last name.

When searching through library catalogs students may have more options than just conducting a keyword search. To narrow a search, books may be searched by author, title or both. In some instances the search could involve locating materials centered on a particular reading level.

When conducting any search it helps if the researcher is familiar with the capabilities and limitations of the resource being used.

Skill 5.4 Demonstrating knowledge of methods for conducting print-based and electronic searches (e.g., using key words, subject headings, cross-references, Boolean operators), for evaluating the progress of a search(e.g., reexamining gathered information), and for adjusting search strategies in response to search results

Information retrieval is the process of searching, recovering and interpreting information from large amounts of stored data. Below are the basic steps involved in successful information retrieval.

When searching for information the researcher first begins with the topic. Write down words or phrases that directly relate to the topic being covered. Start with general terms and then break them down into more specific areas. These terms become the keywords that will be used in the search. A keyword is an important word or phrase that is used to retrieve information.

Once the set of keywords have been determined, use them to search books, articles or electronic resources. When searching through print materials the researcher will look for specific subject headings. Subject headings are words or phrases that are used to locate resources by topics. When information can be found under more than one subject heading, the information is often cross-referenced. The words "See also" may be used to direct the researcher to a more appropriate heading.

With the vast amount of information available to library patrons it is important that they know how to locate information quickly and easily. Whether using in-house resources such as an automated circulation systems and CD-ROM database or searching for information online, effective search strategies must be employed.

The main type of search is a keyword search where the user searches for information using specific terms. To aid in this type of search certain operators called Boolean Operators can narrow topics. Popular operators include:

- AND – eg. Lions AND tigers – commands the search engine to find both words in the searched text.
- AND – eg. Lions AND tigers – commands the search engine to find both words in the searched text.
- AND NOT – eg. Lions AND NOT tigers – commands the search engine to find texts that list lions but to ignore texts that list tigers.
- OR – eg. Lions OR tigers – commands the search engine top find texts that contain either word.

When conducting a search it may be necessary to modify search strategies or parameters in order to narrow the results or to find more relevant information. One of the first places to begin is by analyzing the results that have been returned. Are their certain references that you do not want that continuously appear in the search? Is the specific topic appearing?

When searches are not progressing well, the user usually experiences there types of results . The user will receive too many records, too few records, or no relevant records.

When too many records are returned the user may need to narrow his or her topic by making it more specific. Using Boolean strategies to eliminate unnecessary returns can also make a difference. Another strategy would be to put key phrases in quotation marks so that the terms would be listed together.

When a search returns too few records it may be necessary to broaden the search, as the topic may have been too narrow. Take a look at any relevant records that were returned and evaluate the descriptors to locate potential terms to add to the search.

If no relevant records are returned, check the spelling of the search topic or look for the information in a different source.

Skill 5.5　　Identifying strategies for helping students learn methods to locate and access information efficiently and independently

For students to be truly information literate they need to be armed with strategies that will guide them through the abundance of resources they are able to access. Their independence evolves as they:

- learn to develop essential questions,
- identify the keywords needed to locate information,
- evaluate the information that is found,
- and find creative ways to share their information.

This evolution can often occur as students partake in reference requests. There are three types of reference requests depending on the depth of the question and the scope of the search. However, some very simple questions can lead to complex searches.

1. Ready reference request. These requests usually require a limited search in standard reference books (e.g., encyclopedias, atlases, almanacs, etc.) or electronic databases (e.g., *SIRS Researcher*, *Grolier's Encyclopedia*, *3D Atlas*, or *American Heritage Dictionary and Thesaurus*). The request is satisfied by directing the requestor to the exact sources in which the information may be found. Occasionally, a seemingly simple question cannot be answered quickly and thus necessitates a higher level search.
   If the library carries the *Who's Who in America* and *Who Was Who in America* series, an American is easy to identify. However, most school library media centers do not purchase biographical dictionaries of foreign persons unless they were noteworthy in a particular profession. *Who's Who in Science, Current Biography, Webster's Biographical Dictionary, British Writers Before 1900,* etc. are some helpful resources.

2. Specific need requests. These requests are the most frequently addressed and may range from merely steering the requestor to a card catalog, index or other bibliographic aid if the user is familiar with those tools. Specific needs requests are especially useful if students are working on a lengthy project and resources must be found outside the school, and the user may need instruction in using search tools and locating the resources.

   A student debater may want to know which resources would give statistics about teen pregnancy. A teacher may ask which books and periodicals have the best articles on inclusion of special education students.

   The answer to specific need questions entails locating the resources by identifying the proper search tools (e.g., card catalog, the *Reader's Guide to Periodical Literature*, or automated indexes like *Infotrac* or *Newsbank*).

3. Research request. This question is encountered most often in secondary school, university and academic libraries. The search is broader in scope and requires more time. Any specific need request could be expanded into a research request.

A debater may be preparing a portfolio for a contest and needs photocopies of available material. A teacher taking a college course may ask the school library media specialist to pull periodical articles relating to inclusion. These requests may require using on-line databases and research queries outside the library media center. Research services are gaining wider need as users are confronted with great amounts of information as they have less time to conduct their searches.

COMPETENCY 6.0 UNDERSTAND STRATEGIES FOR EVALUATING INFORMATION AND COMMUNICATING INFORMATION OBTAINED FROM A SEARCH.

Skill 6.1 Identifying strategies for locating potentially useful information (e.g., previewing, skimming, scanning) and applying criteria for evaluating information (e.g., currency, purpose, authority, accuracy, objectivity, scope)

As students begin to search for information resources for research or other projects it is important to evaluate the resources selected for their effectiveness.

One of the main sets of strategies to teach students to use when identifying relevant information is to preview, skim and scan information. With this strategy students preview a work by skimming through the book and scanning the chapter titles, headings, charts, images and other diagrams for relevant information to determine quickly as to whether or not they need to read further.

Once a book has met the skim and scan test, there are other factors to consider when looking at any type of resource, whether a book or web page.

These criteria include:

1. Audience: Who was this information intended to reach? What is the level of the information?
2. Scope: How detailed is the information? Is this work focused on an overall outline of the topic or does it provide in depth information on one specific aspect of the topic?
3. When was the information published? How often is the website updated?
4. Who is the author? What authority does this person have to be writing this article?
5. Is the article free from bias? Is it from a single person or an organization trying to argue for a certain position?
6. Does the author include a resource bibliography?
7. Does the information come from a scholarly source or from a popular source?

Skill 6.2   Demonstrating knowledge of strategies for summarizing, organizing and synthesizing information and for drawing appropriate conclusions

Bloom's Taxonomy reminds us that students need to develop higher level thinking skills beyond the basic recollection of facts. For students to understand how to work with information once it is received, three key skills must be in place.

The first skill is the ability to summarize, and this skill is covered in the second level of Bloom's Taxonomy called "Comprehension." By summarizing information students show that they have comprehended the material and can restate key facts.

The second skill is the ability to organize information, also found on the fourth level of Bloom's list under "Analysis." Using this skill, the student takes the information presented and begins to categorize, compare and contrast it.

The third skill is the ability to synthesize information, and this appears just above "Analysis" on Bloom's Taxonomy. When information is synthesized it is collected, developed and further organized so that it can be used for creating a cogent product.

Skill 6.3   Demonstrating knowledge of strategies for presenting information in a form that communicates clearly what has been learned

In the last twenty years, audio-visual materials, once considered supplementary to classroom work, have integral parts of the instructional process. In order to broaden their ability to present information with clarity, students and teachers should take advantage of their instructional media resources. Not only should they use commercial products to design and produce their own materials, but they should also design and produce their own materials.

It is appropriate for faculty to produce their own resources when:

1. Commercial products are unavailable, unsuited to learning styles/preferences/environments, or too costly.
2. Teaching styles indicate a preference for non-commercial products.
3. Teachers have the expertise and necessary equipment for original production.

It is appropriate for students to produce their own resources when:

1. Challenged to achieve understanding with non-verbal means of expression.
2. Communicating ideas and information to others.
3. Expressing creativity.
4. Demonstrating mastery of lesson objectives by alternative means.

Having determined that it is appropriate to use media produced my students or teachers, it is necessary to determine which media should be produced to meet the specific instructional need. School library media specialists may produce media for two purposes:

1. To make presentations for information skills instruction, other teacher-directed activities, or testing.
2. To make materials to be placed directly in the hands of students.

Skill 6.4   Demonstrating knowledge of considerations in selecting an appropriate format (e.g., print, audio, video, multimedia) to communicate information

Many excellent books on media instruction detail the instructional uses of media formats. These uses are largely contingent on the goals of a given lesson or activity. Here are two goals for a lesson along with the suggestions for media that will accomplish with these goals.

1. **Introduction.** Several formats allow large group listening or viewing and are appropriate for introducing new materials. These formats include filmstrips, films, slidetapes, computer projection, overhead transparencies and videotapes. These formats can require a large screen, an elevated monitor or multiple units for viewing. With young learners who are non-readers, display boards with large print and audiocassettes for story-telling are most effective.
2. **Application.** During this phase, media that lend themselves to individual or small group use are needed. As students investigate the subject matter, organize that information, practice, or demonstrate understanding, they may create any or several types of media. With young children these would include manipulatives (e.g., building blocks, letters, numbers or shapes formed with cloth, plastic or wood). Older students would create photographs/slides, audiocassette tapes or videotapes. Some secondary students might even design their own computer programs. Students at all levels can be taught to use computer design software to create multi-media productions.

The introduction and application of media production techniques helps the user, whether child or adult, clarify his or her own objectives and determine the exact format which would best present the ideas and achieve selected goals. A lesson on distinguishing the calls of local birds might introduce the material using audiocassette tapes while recognizing plumage would use slides or videotape. Students preparing a study of estuarine ecology might incorporate video and computer graphics designed from electron microscope imagery to demonstrate their applied knowledge of the various micro-organisms in the local river.

Skill 6.5 Applying knowledge of guidelines for preparing a bibliography or other necessary documentation

Citing resources used for research or student projects is an important part of teaching students about copyright and fair use of information. When citing resources it is best to follow the preferred format of the instructor. There are many online tools that can assist students with this process. Given their field of study, most researches use one of three popular formats.

MLA – Modern Language Association
With this style, you briefly cite the source by placing key information in parenthesis before the punctuation at the end of a sentence (White 95).

The works credited in the bibliography are listed alphabetically by the author's last name using the following format.

White, Joe. "Sample Article." *Sample Magazine* 25 Nov. 2002: 92.

APA – American Psychological Association

When the author is not mentioned with a quote the format would read, (White, 1976, p. 56)

The reference listing would look similar to this:

Author, Joe. (Year of publication). *Title of work: Capital letter for subtitle.* Location: Publisher

Chicago Manual of Style
In text, the reference would be: (White 1999)

The reference listing would be:

Author, Joe. 1998. *The title of the book in lower case: subtitle in lower case.* Publication City: Publisher.

Skill 6.6 **Identifying strategies for helping students learn how to evaluate information and for helping students adopt effective and creative approaches to communicating information**

Evaluation revolves around a student's ability to judge the value of information based on specific criteria. The criteria may focus on the organization of information or the relevance of the information, but the criteria may also be defined by the learning activity itself.

An evaluation may involve specific criterion outlined in a rubric. A rubric is a scoring guide for projects that may be subjective, and students can use the rubric to determine how well they have met the criteria or answered essential questions.

When the project involves specific bits of information used to prove a point or complete an experiment, students can analyze the results to see if the information they gathered met their needs. By interpreting information discovered in the evaluation process students can draw conclusions and begin to take a specific position or determine potential outcomes based upon their information.

COMPETENCY 7.0 UNDERSTAND METHODS AND MATERIALS FOR PROMOTING LEARNING AND INFORMATION LITERACY SKILLS.

Skill 7.1 Demonstrating familiarity with human development, learning theory and instructional design in relation to teaching information literacy skills

Curriculum is defined as the specific skills or objectives students should know or be able to perform when they complete a certain grade level. Most curriculum development takes place at a state level, but local districts may work to develop curriculum specific to local goals and populations.

The process generally works through a team approach utilizing classroom teachers known for their expertise in a particular subject. This team will review current learning objectives and determine their validity or identify changes that need to be made to the curriculum as a whole.

Once changes have been identified they are written as student learning outcomes or goals. A goal is a general statement that is broken down into skills that are needed to meet the goal. Specific examples regarding the mastery of the skill may be provided.

Every goal and skill that is listed must be capable of being measured. The curriculum development process may also include the designing of appropriate assessments to measure a student's level of performance with regards to the skill.

When writing objectives, they must be stated so that the reader is able to determine the intended learner, what the learner will be expected to do (generally phrased using an action verb), the circumstance in which learning will occur, and the degree to which it will be accomplished. Each of these parts must be measurable.

Evaluation of the curriculum is the most crucial step in the process. Through evaluation the new content is measured for effectiveness. After careful evaluation the goal or skill may once again be revised to promote the lifelong learning process for students.

The key factor in curriculum development is that is an ongoing process. Goals and skills must be continuously evaluated for effectiveness and restructured to ensure student success.

Skill 7.2 Demonstrating knowledge of methods for assessing learner needs, instructional methodologies and information processes

To determine the informational needs of a patron it may be necessary to conduct a reference interview. The reference interview is a dialogue between the media specialist and the patron. It should be conducted in a relaxed manner and not feel like an interrogation.

The interview should begin with open-ended questions that cannot be answered with just a yes or no. These questions require a person to be more specific, and as the questioning often begins with general questions that grow more specific as the media specialist uncovers the patron's needs. Types of open-ended interview questions would include:

- What type of information are you searching for?
- What is your topic?
- How much information do you need?
- What information do you have already?
- How will you use this information?
- When do you need to have the information

To further assist patrons the media specialist will also need to ask some closed-end questions that can be answered with a yes or no. Types of relevant closed-end questions include:

- Have you searched the card catalog?
- Do you need World Wide Web sites as well?
- Is this for a class assignment?

It may be more difficult to determine the needs of some patrons. There are variables that can affect the progress of an interview.

- Patron familiarity with resources and how to locate them.
- Age of patron.
- Patron's knowledge of the type of information he or she needs.
- How comfortable the patron feels in asking for assistance.

While questioning and advising a patron, the media specialist should remember the goal of providing safe learning environment for all. In doing so, the specialist should treat all patrons with the utmost courtesy.

Skill 7.3 **Demonstrating knowledge of methods for designing information skills instruction that is based on student interest and learning needs that are linked to the goal of student achievement**

This objective can be best achieved if there are existing scope and sequences in other curricular areas. Information skills, like any other content, should not be taught in isolation if they are to be retained and practiced. If no printed sequences exist, consult with teachers and/or team leaders about planning activities cooperatively to teach information and content skills concurrently.

Teaming with teachers will also meet their instructional objectives. Media specialists need to match resources to those objectives as well as suggest means for using media to demonstrate student skills' mastery. Achievement of the design of resource-based teaching units with supplemental or total involvement of the library media center resources and services satisfy levels 9 and 10 of Loertscher's eleven levels taxonomy. This assumes the active involvement of the school library media specialist in the total school program.

Finally, the self-esteem of students and teachers who learn information management skills is as significant as the information acquisition.

A suggested procedure for incorporation follows:

Preparation:

1. Secure any printed scope and sequences from content areas.

2. Meet with team leaders or department chairs early in the year to plan an integrated, sequential program.

3. Attend department or grade-level meetings with specific time devoted to orienting teachers to available resources and services.

4. Plan best time to schedule orientations for entry level students and reviews for reinforcement.

Implementation:

1. Conduct planned lessons. Distribute copies of objectives, activities, and resources.

2. Review search strategies and challenge students to broaden their scope of resources used to locate information.

3. Provide adequate time for students to carry out lesson activities using media center resources.

Evaluation:

1. Solicit feedback from both students and teachers.

2. Incorporate suggestions into lesson plans.

The International Society of Technology in Education has developed National Educational Technology Standards (NETS) that outline information literacy skills.

To summarize these skills:
- Student should have quick and easy access to information.
- Students should learn to be critical evaluators of information.

Students should be able to utilize information resourcefully.

Skill 7.4   Identifying techniques of incorporating authentic learning opportunities into the library media program

Authentic learning activities have students explore curricular objectives in the context of real world problems and projects that are of interest the student.

Authentic learning activities can be student or teacher driven. One example of such a project is as follows:

The local community holds a strawberry festival each year and is interested in having students assist with advertising the festival. Students can choose to create a website, flyer, radio and/or television ad, or brochure.

To prepare for the creation of their ad, students research the history of the community's festival and learn more about growing and using strawberries. Once the research is gathered, they prepare and distribute their final products.

Authentic learning experiences are more meaningful to students. They feel as if their work is going towards some cause or effort and will really be utilized.

To make these types of experiences successful, the media specialist can help the teacher to develop guidelines, locate effective resources, assist students with research, train students to use relevant technologies, and help oversee the preparation of their final product.

Skill 7.5 Demonstrating knowledge of various teaching strategies and activities for encouraging critical and creative thinking and for promoting information literacy skills, including reading, listening, and viewing skills

Critical thinking skills are essential for academic success and lifelong learning skills. Too often, students simply accept the information presented to them. The media specialist plays an important role in introducing and developing critical thinking skills by providing students with the tools to question not only the assumptions of others, but their own ideas, thoughts and established opinions as well.

Since many students prefer to absorb information without questioning its origin, usefulness, bias or purpose, the media specialist can implement several strategies and activities to counteract this tendency and increase both critical thought and retention.

When developing critical thinking skills, encourage activities such as group discussion, summary writing, thesis identification, or drawing conclusions using supporting evidence. Encourage statements of opinion, assumptions, or observation. You will find students respond differently to instructional methods, which is why it's important to have a full arsenal of critical thinking skill activities available.

Work the teachers to develop and coordinate ongoing critical thinking activities, such as having students research and then present both sides of an issue. Encourage the exploration of age-appropriate questions such as "What do I think about this topic? Why? What more would I wish to learn? How did I arrive at my conclusion or observation?"

Skill 7.6 **Recognizing techniques for creating instructional materials that encourage student learning and reading (e.g., audio, photos, videos, displays, bulletin boards, charts, electronic media)**

As the media special prepares to create instructional media, there are three primary stages that will help to maximize student reading and learning. The first is the planning stage. Here are some recommended steps for the planning stage.

1. State the main idea (goal) of the production, clearly and concisely.
2. Determine the purpose of the product.
   a. To provide information or develop appreciation. Media with this purpose is general in nature, usually meant for presentation to a class or larger group acting as passive listeners. However, it must use dramatic or motivational appeals to hold audience interest.
   b. To provide instruction. Designed for individual or small group use, instructive media should be specific, systematic and interactive.
3. Develop the objectives. State specifically what the audience should know or be able to do after using this media and what measurements will be used to determine their knowledge or ability.
4. Analyze the audience. Determine ability and interest, learning styles, and current understanding of the topic.
5. Research the idea. Use print, non-print and human resources to study both the subject matter and the media techniques/formats to best present the subject matter.

Once a plan is created, the next stage is to design the material:

1. Prepare an outline of the content. Create story board cards for each subheading and match them to the objectives.
2. Select the media format(s) to communicate the idea. Consider time, effort and cost as well as audio-visual needs. If motion and sound are not essential, consider using transparencies or slides since they are easier to make and require no editing. Consider the equipment and facilities available.
3. Create the content. Prepare a story board delineating the description of each graphic and write a corresponding script if captions or sound narration will be included.
4. Create the media.

Once the materials are designed, the media specialist will want to evaluate the effectiveness of the materials as they are presented to the group. Evaluation is the final stage for creating and implementing instructional media. Here are some tips for evaluating materials:

1. Observe reaction of audience to resources. Body language and verbal reactions, especially in younger children, will indicate the level of interest.
2. Solicit verbal or written reactions to appearance, arrangement, and technical quality as well as ease of understanding and mastery of content.
3. Examine costs. Determine if costs of materials and time invested were equal to outcomes.

COMPETENCY 8.0 UNDERSTAND THE CHARACTERISTICS OF EFFECTIVE TEACHERS OF INFORMATION LITERACY SKILLS.

Skill 8.1 Identifying strategies for working in partnership with classroom teachers and other educators to plan, deliver and evaluate information skills instruction

One of the single most important parts of a successful leadership of a school library media program is collaboration between the school library media specialist and classroom teachers.

To support the collaborative process there are key skills the media specialist must possess. These include:
- **Flexibility** to adjust to the differing logistical and scheduling needs of staff and students.
- **Expertise** in the curriculum being taught at the grade levels being served. This makes the media specialist and invaluable collaborative partner.
- **Leadership** will set the goals for and expectations of the media program should move towards. Strong leadership skills will also help the specialist be the advocate for the teachers as well as the media program
- **Approachability** establishes good rapport with staff and students. The specialist should establish a reputation of being one who takes the extra step for teachers and students.
- **Persistence** to keep going and keep the media program moving forward

Skill 8.2 Applying knowledge of the advantages and limitations of various instructional strategies and assessment tools for given educational goals or objectives

Despite the diversity of responsibilities, a school library media specialist is first and foremost a teacher. The percentage of time devoted to structured teaching activities is greater in elementary school, especially if the media center is still on rigid scheduling. As students mature, structured lessons should be shortened and followed by longer hands-on activities for reinforcement of the learned skills.

Several factors have contributed to defining the school library media specialist's instructional role. These include:

1. Introduction of pre-kindergarten programs into elementary schools. As more public schools have introduced PK programs, many states have expanded certification parameters. However, training in understanding that age group and its unique needs has not kept pace. One survey indicated that most certified media specialists considered parenthood their best qualification for dealing with preschoolers.

2. Greater emphasis on developing higher order thinking skills. Even in primary grades, students are encouraged to synthesize information and make media productions to present the results of their learning. Middle school students should be reading critically and making value judgments about the quality of their reading material.
3. Cooperative planning and learning. Research affirms that information skills instruction must be integrated into the curriculum. Furthermore, the days of silence in libraries has given way to learning noise, students working in groups and producing necessary communication. Working in teams gives the students preparation for the real work world.

At all levels, library media specialists should be expected to complete the following:

1. Train students in information location using traditional and new information retrieval skills.
2. Facilitate students' understanding of different media formats and the purpose of various information presentation formats.
3. Assist students in developing critical thinking skills in relation to the located information.
4. Reinforce library media citizenship skills.
5. Teach information skills.

Once the media specialist has completed his or her part as a classroom instructor, the specialist should be prepared to assess the students. The various methods of assessment include:

1. Evaluating students' reading habits by use of student surveys or interviews, by packaged assessment programs like Accelerated Reader, or by some in-house record keeping system. Several good standardized tests exist for testing reading progression.
2. Evaluating visual literacy by observing students' own visual designs (e.g., drawings, graphic designs, photographs, motion pictures and computer graphics). Students must also be able to present a verbal analysis of various images they perceive and to interpret the messages delivered.
3. Evaluating listening skills by observing the student's ability to follow oral directions, to remember facts and details, and to retell information. Standardized or teacher-made tests can be implemented to pre-test and post-test the mastery of listening skills.
4. Evaluating media literacy by observing students' use of equipment needed to create productions and noting the final product of media projects for appropriateness of format, length and depth of coverage, graphic quality, focus, etc.

For more information on this, please see Skill 7.3.

Skill 8.3 **Demonstrating knowledge of strategies for encouraging students to use information skills to solve problems, pursue knowledge and explore the world of information for personal interest and self-improvement**

Information literacy can be defined as the capability to understand when information is needed and to identify, evaluate and use the information effectively. Such literacy combines what we already know with the skills needed to thrive in the future. With the increased access to information that is possible because of technology, it is crucial for learners to not only be able to locate information but to distinguish between that which is valid or that which is not.

There are many information literacy models. One of the most commonly used is the Big6 model created by educators Mike Eisenberg and Bob Berkowitz. The Big6 process outlines how people solve an information problem. Eisenberg and Berkowitz have broken down this process into six stages that a specialist can use to encourage students to solve problems with their information skills.

1. **Task Definition** – identify problem and information needed
2. **Information Seeking Strategies** – decide on sources of information and select the best
3. **Location and Access** – locate the sources and search for the information
4. **Use of Information** – interact with the information and pick out that which is most relevant
5. **Synthesis** – organize the information and present it
6. **Evaluation** – evaluate effectiveness of the product and the process

Another popular model includes Pathways to Knowledge Information Skills Model. It was created by Professor Marjorie Pappas and Ann Tepe, Follett Software's Director of Curriculum. This model outlines strategies that include appreciation, pre-search, search, interpretation, communication and evaluation.

Skill 8.4 **Applying knowledge of strategies for selecting resources, including technological resources, to support students with diverse learning abilities, styles and needs**

Schools today serve a very diverse population of students including those from various cultural and socioeconomic backgrounds along with those that have physical and learning disabilities. It is of the utmost importance that the school library media programs provide resources and technologies that help all students gain access to information.

Resources must come in a wide variety of formats including: large print books, audio books, video books, and Braille texts.

Technology has made it easier for students with physical and learning disabilities to learn. Software such as the Kurzweil Reader can read scanned pages or online text to students with reading difficulties. There are also many devices that help students with limited language abilities or mobility, and these types of devices are called assistive or adaptive technology.

Assistive technology is any device that helps someone with a disability perform a task that he or she may not be able to accomplish alone. These devices can include: joysticks, keyboard overlays or extensions, optical pointing devices, touch screens, Braille displays and embossers and screen enhancement functions.

Since school library media specialists teach all children within a school, every child should have the right resources to insure individual success.

Skill 8.5 Recognizing methods for maintaining regular communication between the school library media center and students, their families and the community

When attempting to maintain communication with the school and its community, recognize the many technology tools that will save time and increase productivity. The types of applications available will be determined by district adopted software. Examples of types of productivity tools and their uses include:

- **Word processing software** – most effective for creating letters, reports, simple brochures and flyers.
- **Desktop publishing software** – similar to word processing, but is designed to accommodate more complicated layouts for newsletters, brochures, cards and certificates.
- **Electronic calendars** – generally allow the users to share calendars with others, post and view appointments online. Since these are typically web-based, they can be viewed anywhere.
- **Spreadsheets** – effective in managing media budgets. Spreadsheets can be used to track purchases and balances from multiple funding sources.
- **Databases** – effective for organizing, managing and retrieving resources. Databases can be used for collection management and managing inventory.
- **Presentation Software** – multimedia presentations are effective tools for promoting the media program by sharing information with others.
- **Web Applications** – web pages can be created using simple html editors, WYSIWYG (What You See Is What You Get) software, or more complicated programs that create animations and interactive sites.
- **Teleconferencing software** – allows users to communicate over the Internet using audio and/or video.

Most productivity tools come packaged in software sets purchased by a school district. Apple Productivity Tools, Microsoft Office, and Lotus are also examples of software sets that may include word processing, spreadsheets, databases and multimedia applications.

Skill 8.6 **Recognizing the benefits of self-reflection as a path to professional growth**

Self-reflection is meant to be a process to guide a teacher through an examination of previous activities and to propose improvements for the future. Observations gleaned from self-reflection can serve as a starting point for professional development plans.

Possible questions for self-reflection are:
- In what instructional areas have you seen growth this year?
- What has been one of your most successful activities? Why?
- What curriculum areas have been most challenging for your students this year?
- What adjustments did you make in your teaching approach to assist students with learning these concepts?
- What have been the most valuable pieces of information gained from professional development activities you've participated in this year?
- How has that information changed the way you teach?
- Describe your overall rapport with your students. Describe specific incidents that you were successful in meeting student needs.
- How would you describe your relationship with the faculty and staff at your school?

SUBAREA III.	COLLABORATION AND LEADERSHIP IN THE LIBRARY MEDIA CONTEXT

COMPETENCY 9.0 UNDERSTAND THE ROLE OF THE MEDIA SPECIALIST IN CURRICULUM DEVELOPMENT

Skill 9.1 Demonstrating knowledge of basic principles of curriculum development and standardized practices

Curriculum is defined as the specific skills or objectives students should know or be able to perform when they complete a certain grade level. Most curriculum development takes place at a state level, but local districts may work to develop curriculum specific to local goals and populations.

The process generally works through a team approach utilizing classroom teachers known for their expertise in a particular subject. This team will review current learning objectives and determine their validity or identify changes that need to be made to the curriculum as a whole.

Once changes have been identified they are written as student learning outcomes or goals. A goal is a general statement that is broken down into skills that are needed to meet the goal. Specific examples regarding the mastery of the skill may be provided.

Every goal and skill that is listed must be capable of being measured. The curriculum development process may also include the designing of appropriate assessments to measure a student's level of performance with regards to the skill.

When writing objectives, they must be stated so that the reader is able to determine the intended learner, what the learner will be expected to do (generally phrased using an action verb), the circumstance in which learning will occur, and the degree to which it will be accomplished. Each of these parts must be measurable.

Evaluation of the curriculum is the most crucial step in the process. Through evaluation the new content is measured for effectiveness. After careful evaluation the goal or skill may once again be revised to promote the lifelong learning process for students.

The key factor in curriculum development is that is an ongoing process. Goals and skills must be continuously evaluated for effectiveness and restructured to ensure student success.

TEACHER CERTIFICATION STUDY GUIDE

Skill 9.2 **Recognizing the importance of participating in district, building, departmental and grade level curriculum design and assessment projects**

The school library media specialist plays a vital role in curriculum design and directing the vision of a school. In the publication, *School Library Programs: Standards and Guidelines*, there is a strong emphasis on the importance of collaboration between the library media specialist and the classroom teacher. This collaboration should include involvement on school and district curriculum committees.

As a team member, the school library media specialist contributes by completing the following:

1. Advising of current trends and studies in curriculum design.
2. Advising the school staff on the use of media and instructional techniques to meet learning objectives.
3. Ensuring that a systematic approach to information skills instruction will be included in curriculum plans.
4. Recommending media and technologies appropriate to particular subject matter and activities.

Skill 9.3 **Identifying strategies for engaging in cooperative planning with faculty and others to ensure that information literacy skills are integrated into the curriculum**

To begin the cooperative or collaborative planning process with teachers it is often beneficial to start with those teachers who may be most willing to engage in the process. The process can be formal or informal, but the focus should be related to the integration of information literacy skills.

One of the first parts of the process is to identify essential question that outline what the teacher wants the students to know and be able to do.

The next part of the process involves determining the information literacy skills that will be used during the completion of the activity or lesson.

From here the teacher and media specialist determine activities and assessments. Then they gather possible resources such as technology, materials and assistance that may be needed.

Skill 9.4 Recognizing methods for collaborating with classroom teachers to promote interdisciplinary learning

The American Library Association lists four models for collaboration.

Model A – Coordination – This is the least intense model that focuses on working together to smooth out the instructional process, but it does not necessarily focus on student outcomes.

Model B – Cooperation/Partnership – Requiring more commitment than the first, this model involves two or more entities defining and working towards specific goals and objectives. This type of interaction can be used to develop trust and build working relationships.

Model C – Integrated Instruction – In this model the teacher and librarian work closely in all aspects including planning, designing and evaluation. There is a deep level of trust with this relationship as the teacher and librarian work together to create a quality learning experience for the students. Each participant shares their expertise in the subject content, knowledge of standards and various learning processes. The librarian and teacher are able to create a more meaningful learning activity together than they could have created alone.

Model D – Integrated Curriculum – This model pulls together all of the points from Model C but incorporates collaboration into the entire curriculum. A key factor for this model is that there is strong administrative support for the collaborative process. The principal recognizes the importance of the partnership between the classroom and the media program and provides opportunities for the process to be used to its fullest potential.

Skill 9.5 Applying knowledge of methods for collaborating with staff in selecting and acquiring resources to support curricular needs

One of the most important ways to align resources is for the media specialist to collaborate closely with classroom teachers. This collaboration can take the form of:

- serving on curriculum development committees at all levels in order to integrate information literacy and provide instructional resources;
- working jointly with teachers as partners in the planning, designing, teaching and evaluating of instructional activities;
- assisting both teachers and students in the effective use of instructional technologies;
- and establishing the integration of information literacy skills across the curriculum.

Skill 9.6   Applying knowledge of academic performance standards in selecting and acquiring resources to support curricular needs

The school library media specialist must do their best to familiarize themselves with the curriculum covered within the school. A library media and technology advisory committee comprised of teachers from each grade of subject can hold the expertise which the media specialist relies upon. Understanding curriculum is necessary to ensure the media collection meets the needs of the user.

Ways to determine needed resources can include:

- Creating a collection map that identifies the resources found under each Dewey section.
- Surveying staff regarding needs.
- Meeting with teachers to determine needs.
- Collaborating closely with the teacher. A collaborative relationship allows the media specialist to stay abreast of curricular projects and what teachers need to accomplish them.

COMPETENCY 10.0 UNDERSTAND THE ROLE OF THE MEDIA SPECIALIST AS AN INSTRUCTIONAL PARTNER.

Skill 10.1 Demonstrating knowledge of current trends and issues in education and of research indicating the relationship between the school library media program and improved student achievement

The American Library Association lists the top trends for library media programs as the following:

1. Internet Use in Libraries

   It is important that library media specialists embrace the potential of the Internet. The abundance of resources can open doors and expand the smallest collection. Because of the overabundance of information that may be deemed inappropriate for young children, many specialists often shy away from its use. A media specialist who is well educated in Internet resources is a valuable asset for any school.

2. The Librarian's Changing Role

   Technology has drastically changed the way librarians run their media programs. They have become the manager of a wealth of information both in print and online.

3. Developing Partnerships with Outside Entities

   It is crucial for libraries to develop partnerships with outside resources. Such partnerships help libraries save money by limiting the amount of funds dedicated to building collections. Whether partnering with schools in their own district or with independent universities and museums, there is great benefit to students in regards to the breadth and depth of available resources.

4. Protecting Patron Privacy

   Libraries have taken a strong stand in the protection of the privacy rights of their patrons. Through many recent historical developments this is becoming an ever-increasing issue, especially when it comes to patron Internet usage.

5. Electronic Books

   The management of electronic books is an issue more and more libraries are facing. Rules for check-out and copyright concerns are a few of the topics taking shape with electronic books.

Skill 10.2 **Demonstrating knowledge of techniques for collaborating with teachers in the development of instructional strategies, activities and assessments to guide students in developing a full range of information literacy and communication abilities**

The American Library Association has outlined four major models of collaboration, as described in Skill 9.4. The ideal collaborative relationship is Model D – Integrated Curriculum. With this model the media specialist is truly an extension of the classroom teacher. The two continuously work together to create quality lessons complete with assessments to develop information literacy skills.

As part of this process the media specialists incorporate information literacy models such as Big6 or ISearch. These models focus upon identifying topics, locating resources, evaluating that information and presenting the material.

Skill 10.3 **Demonstrating knowledge of methods and materials for instructing and training members of the school learning community in the use of information resources and technologies**

The design of a staff development activity is similar to a basic lesson profile with accommodations and special considerations for adult learners. The following steps should used when planning and implementing training for members of the school learning community.

1. Analyze learner styles. Adult learners are more receptive to role playing and individual performance before a group. Learner motivation is more internal, but some external motivations, such as release time, compensatory time, in service credit or some written recognition, might be discussed with the principal.
2. Assess learner needs. Conduct a survey among teachers to determine which media or equipment they want to learn more about. Consider environmental factors such as time, place and temperature. Since many in service activities occur after school, taking the lesson to the teachers in their own classrooms may make them more comfortable especially if they can have a reviving afternoon snack. If they must come to the media center, serve refreshments.
3. Select performance objectives. Determine exactly what the teacher should be able to do at the end of a successful in service session.
4. Plan activities to achieve objectives. Demonstrate the skill to be taught, involve the participants in active performance and production, and allow for practice and feedback.
5. Select appropriate resources. Arrange that all materials and equipment are ready and in good functioning order on the day of the in service.

6. Determine instructor. Either the school library media specialist or a faculty member should conduct these on-site in services unless the complexity or novelty of the technology requires an outside expert.
7. Provide continuing support. This support is the key to making staff development effective. Staff are most likely to continue to use what they've learned when they know they will be able to receive assistance with implementation. The instructor or designated substitute should be available after the in service for reinforcement.
8. Evaluation. Determine the effectiveness of the in service and make modifications as recommended in future in services.

Skill 10.4 Identifying strategies for working with members of the learning community to share information, engage in action research and apply research results

To improve student learning it is often necessary to engage in research that examines current teaching strategies and searches for ways to improve upon them. This type of research is known as action research. Most often, teachers determine the focus topic to be examined. The process is not as formal as other research formats, yet it can provide the most valuable results with regards to improving their teaching.

The process includes:
1. Determining the focus
2. Developing a plan. Decide upon the timeline, the information to be gathered and the format in which the information will be gathered.
3. Analyze the information by determining themes that arise.
4. Summarize what has been learned

Media specialists can play a key role in the process by helping to determine topics of study and by providing or developing tools such as surveys, questionnaires or spreadsheets to assist with data collection.

COMPETENCY 11.0 UNDERSTAND THE ROLE OF THE MEDIA SPECIALIST AS AN EDUCATIONAL LEADER.

Skill 11.1 Demonstrating basic knowledge of leadership strategies, expectations and goals

A good leader should be able to work and inspire others to work in a team environment where the input of team members at all levels is encouraged and appreciated. To accomplish this goal, the leader should:

1. Exhibit the desire to achieve the goals of an efficient library media program.
2. Show appreciation for the contributions of library media staff and supervise them in a democratic style.
3. Delegate tasks to responsible staff members.
4. Engage in continuing education.
5. Maintain active membership in professional organizations.
6. Show respect and concern for colleagues and superiors.

One of the single most important parts of a successful leadership of a school library media program is collaboration between the school library media specialist and classroom teachers.

To support the collaborative process there are key skills the media specialist must possess. These include:

- **Flexibility** to adjust to the differing logistical and scheduling needs of staff and students.
- **Expertise** in the curriculum being taught at the grade levels being served. This makes the media specialist and invaluable collaborative partner.
- **Leadership** will set the goals for and expectations of the media program should move towards. Strong leadership skills will also help the specialist be the advocate for the teachers as well as the media program
- **Approachability** establishes good rapport with staff and students. The specialist should establish a reputation of being one who takes the extra step for teachers and students.
- **Persistence** to keep going and keep the media program moving forward

Skill 11.2 Recognizing the role of the media specialist in providing leadership and expertise in the use of learning resources and instructional technology

Staff, including teachers and support personnel, should be offered periodic in-service in learning new skills and reinforcing known skills. These skills may be taught at formal, structured workshops or in informal small-group or individual sessions when a need arises. This will inspire all staff members to incorporate instructional media into their lessons and interactions with students.

Sample activities include:

1. A hands-on orientation for teachers new to the school as a means to familiarize them with available resources and apprise them of services. The orientation should include information on incorporating appropriate media into their lessons. Written procedures for selection and evaluation should be available
2. Informational handouts that detail new and existing media. These can also be used to solicit recommendations.
    a. Frequently send bibliographies, catalogs or newsletters, asking for purchase suggestions.
    b. Inform all teachers of district and school preview policies and arrange previews for purchase suggestions.
    c. Involve as many teachers as possible on review committees.
3. Periodically provide brief refresher modules. Advertise the media and equipment to be used in each session. Suggest uses of potential lessons for each media format so teachers can make appropriate choices. Have teachers create one or more products at each session that can be used for instruction in an upcoming lesson.
4. Secure oral or written feedback on both teacher-made and commercial media used in classroom lessons. Ask teachers to use appropriate evaluation criteria in measuring the product's worth. The more familiar they become with the criteria, the better their product choices will become.

Skill 11.3   Identifying strategies for promoting a culture of inquiry within the school community

An effective school library media program can become the heart of learning in any school environment, fostering a culture of inquiry for students and staff alike. A deciding factor in the success of the program is the dedication of the school library media specialist. For a school library media program to be successful it must possess the following characteristics:

- The program must be student-centered. Students have the opportunity to learn to be efficient managers of information. They participate in learning activities that foster creativity and build critical thinking skills. Students collaborate with the school library media specialists to facilitate their learning experiences.
- The program works to expand students' interests and to foster a love of reading, listening and viewing
- It works to provide access to information and assist students in evaluating that information so that it can be used effectively.
- The program assists students in becoming lifelong learners by teaching them to appreciate varying perspectives, act responsibly with regard to information, build critical thinking skills, analyze information and create products based upon the information learned.
- The school library media specialist collaborates with students and staff to provide authentic learning experiences that integrate information skills into the curriculum. Collaboration is one of the most crucial components to the success of a school library media program.
- The school library media specialist works as a leader within the school, bringing resources into the school and training others to use those resources.
- The school library media specialist creates partnerships within the community, further enhancing educational opportunities for students.
- The school library media specialist provides physical access to resources that meets the needs of all populations.

Skill 11.4 Demonstrating knowledge of methods for using the school's mission, goals, policies, structure and culture to advocate for the school library media program

Proper planning is essential to the success of any school library media program. The planning process will take determination, but a quality media program is of great benefit to any school.

For the planning process to be successful, it must have the support of the principal. Include other key people from within the school such as teachers, school support staff, parents, and students. This group of individuals would become part of a school library planning committee that is also known as the Media Advisory Committee (MAC) or Media and Technology Advisory Committee (MTAC). Utilizing such a committee approach is reflective of site-based management where decisions are made by a group of stakeholders or a committee rather than being left to the discretion of one person.

One of the first things the planning committee must do is develop a mission statement that defines the core purpose of the school library media program. The mission statement must become the main focus from which all goals are formed and decisions are made.

The mission of any organization, business or educational institution should evolve from the needs and expectations of its customers. In the case of the school library media center, its mission must parallel the school's mission and attend to the users' needs for resources and services.

The school library media program should examine school and student characteristics.

School:
1. The mission of the school library media center should reflect and be in harmony with the stated school mission.
2. The program's mission should reflect the curricular direction of the school, whether the school is academic, vocational, compensatory.
3. The mission should reflect the willingness of the administration and faculty to support the program.

Student:
1. The mission is influenced by pupil demographics that include age, achievement and ability levels, reading levels, and learning styles.
2. The mission may indicate the students' interest in self-directed learning and exploratory reading.
3. The mission reflects support from parents and community groups.

Once a mission has been defined, it is important to assess the current status of the program and see how closely it follows that mission. Gathering this information is essential to the formation of effective goals and objectives.

It is important to note that evaluation is an ongoing process. It must occur prior to determining goals and objectives and on a regular basis thereafter to ensure they are being met.

A wide variety of evaluation criteria may be used. The criteria may be:

1. Diagnostic. These are standards based on conditions existing in programs that have already been judged as excellent.
2. Projective. These standards are guidelines for conditions as they ought to be.
3. Quantitative. These standards require numerical measurement.
4. Qualitative. These standards are designed to express essentially the measured criteria as quantitative without exact numerical amounts. Action research is a form of qualitative data collection that occurs when educators reflect upon their teaching by observing occurrences in a school or classroom and identifying problems. The educator then devises steps or actions to correct the problem.

Most school library media program evaluations have been diagnostic or qualitative. Diagnostic prescriptions alone make no allowances for specific conditions in given schools and are often interpreted too liberally; in addition, qualitative prescriptions alone are difficult to measure or sustain. Projective standards are usually broad national guidelines which are best used as long-range goals. Preferably, a program evaluation utilizing a combination of quantitative and qualitative standards produces results that can lead to modified objectives. Statistics to substantiate quantitative standards can be derived from:

1. Usage statistics from automated circulation systems. These indicate frequency of materials use.
2. Inventory figures. Resource turnover, loss and damage, and missing materials statistics indicate extent of use. Total materials count can substantiate materials per student criteria.
3. Individual circulation logs. Such logs indicate the frequency of patron use of library materials and the types of materials used.
4. Class scheduling log. Depending on the amount of data acquired when a visit is scheduled, several facts can be determined: proportion of staff and student body using materials and services; the frequency of use of specific resources or services; the age levels of users; specific subgroups being served; and subject matter preferences.

Evidence of meeting qualitative standards can be derived from:

1. **Lesson plans.** Careful planning will reveal the frequency of use of resources and specific classroom objectives planned cooperatively with faculty. The plan should also specify the effectiveness with which the students achieved the lesson objectives.
2. **Personnel evaluations.** Most districts have either formative evaluations, summative evaluations, or both for professional, para-professional, or non-professional staff. Student aides should receive educational credit for their services hours. Completion of specific skills and termination grades can provide both quantitative and qualitative data.
3. **Surveys.** A systematic written evaluation should be conducted annually to obtain input from students, teachers and parents on the success of program objectives.
4. **Conferences / Library Advisory Committee meetings.** Comments from faculty members and students can provide qualitative assessment of the value of the materials and services provided.
5. **Criterion-referenced or teacher made tests**. These assessments can be used to evaluate student effectiveness in acquiring information skills or content area skills.

The purpose of evaluation is to determine if all aspects of planning and implementation have been successfully accomplished. If evaluation shows unsuccessful outcomes, then the program must be modified. Successful outcomes can be used to confirm program objectives and to promote the media center programs.

Some strategies for the use of program evaluation include:

1. To produce an annual report to be included in the school's annual report to parents or other publications for circulation in the community.
2. To review and modify long-range goals and plan immediate changes in short-range goals.
3. To lobby for budgetary or personnel support.
4. To solicit assistance from faculty and administration in making curricular or instructional changes to maximize use of media center materials, equipment and services.
5. To plan greater involvement of students in academic and personal use of media center materials and services.

Because there is currently an abundance of outstanding resource that is easily accessible through technology, evaluation can be managed by following a few simple steps.

1. Rely on the information provided in this guide's resource list. If your school or district's professional library does not contain these resources, visit the public library in the nearest large city or a university library where information sciences are taught.
2. Give your school media program a close examination before doing your research. Study any written evaluations by media personnel, school improvement committees, library advisory committees, or annual reports. Informally survey a cross-section of students and teachers to gather input about their perceptions of the materials and services that are provided.
3. Make a list of questions based on the concerns that result from your evaluation. Peruse the questions in Chapter One of *Information Power* to see if there are any pertinent areas that have not yet been addressed.
4. Do your research.
5. Produce a written evaluation of your school's library media program based on your findings. Submit this evaluation to the principal and plan with her the best way to communicate the information to students, teachers, and parents.
6. Gather input from all groups to whom your evaluation is presented.
7. Meet with the Library Media Advisory Committee or equivalent group to formulate program changes. Be sure to include students and parents or lay community members on this committee.
8. Implement the changes and plan subsequent evaluations.

Once an initial program evaluation has been completed, program goals and objectives may be determined. These goals and objectives help to break down the overall vision for school library media program into areas that the school feels are most important for its successful operation. Some of these goals may already be determined by national or state guidelines that a district's administrators have agreed to maintain. Sometimes, a district operates without a program to guide school library media centers. In that case each school must be responsible not only for setting its own criteria but also for inspiring some district planning.

The first step would be to define major goals (i.e., a long range plan). A goal is a broad statement of an intended outcome that reflects the mission of the school library media program that provides direction. Therefore, when planning a school library media program based on an assessment of school and student characteristics, the program planning team should factor in these elements.

A long-range plan should:

1. Extend from 3-5 years.
2. Incorporate the goals of the other departments (e.g., grade levels or content teams) in the school.
3. Be stated in terms that are non-limiting. The goal should be an achievable aim, not a pipe dream.

Specific goals for school library media centers are outlined in *Information Power: Building Partnerships for Learning.* Key points include:

- providing access to resources and information through integrated activities on a variety of levels,
- providing physical access to a wide variety of resources and information from various locations including outside agencies and electronic resources,
- assisting patrons in locating and evaluating information,
- collaborating with teachers and others,
- facilitating the lifelong learning process,
- building a school library media program that acts as the hub for all learning within the school,
- providing resources that embrace cultural and social differences and support concepts of intellectual freedom

After the major goals have been defined, objectives must be determined. An objective is a specific statement of a measurable result that will occur by a particular time (i.e., it must specify the conditions and criteria to be met effectively.) Objectives reflect short- term priorities, and they must have a specific format. Objectives must contain an action verb and must be measurable. A few of the action verbs often seen in objectives are: discuss, define, compare, identify, explain and design.

A short-range plan should be one part of a longer range plan that is:

1. Accomplishable in one year or less.
2. Linked meaningfully in a logical progression to the expressed goal.
3. Flexible, as most objectives must be processed through affected groups before finalization.

Using an Olympic athlete as an example, an appropriate set of goals and objectives might go as follows:

Goal: To win an Olympic Medal.

Objectives:

1. To increase my speed by .05 seconds per meter by June 30.
2. To double my practice time during the two weeks before the competition begins.
3. To lose 3 lbs. before my weigh-in.

If translated into goals and objectives for library media centers, the set may read as the following:

Goal: To develop a collection more suited to the academic demands of the curriculum

Objectives:

1. To increase non-fiction collection by 10% in the next school year.
2. To ensure readability levels suited to gifted students for 5% of new selections.

Goal: To provide telecommunications services within three years.

Objectives:

1. To design a model for instructional use in 1996.
2. To plan for equipment and facilities needs in 1997.
3. To implement the model with a control group in 1998.

If a school seeks or wishes to maintain accreditation with the Southern Association of Colleges and Schools (SAC), using that organization's recommendations is an excellent way to set program goals and objectives. Because SAC requires every accredited school to conduct an intensive ten year reevaluation and a five year interim review, the library media center program planners may wish to coordinate their own study with SAC's reviews.

Building support for the school library media program creates a network of individuals willing to work to enhance the learning experiences for students. Advocacy always begins with support from a solid program mission.

The American Library Association has developed an Advocacy Toolkit to assist libraries in promoting their programs. Parts of this toolkit include the following:

- The @ Your Library program. This outlines the role of the school library media specialist and the programs they manage.
- Powerpoint presentations that explain @ Your Library and provide topics of discussion.
- An implementation plan for Information Power.
- Brochures for promoting advocacy.
- Guides for meeting with government officials.
- Resource guides for promoting the media center, intellectual freedom and other topics.
- A communication handbook.

Skill 11.5   Demonstrating knowledge of strategies for establishing partnerships with members of the school community to incorporate the library media program into school improvement activities

The school library media program is no longer an isolated entity within a school. One of the most valuable activities specialists can do to promote the library media program is to develop partnerships within the community. Research has shown that strong parental and community involvement can increase student achievement.

When considering the formation of partnerships the school library media specialist must first examine the curriculum for the grade levels it serves as well as the goals for the media program. This will help to determine the people, agencies and organizations that will best help meet student needs.

To begin the process, the school library media specialist must contact the agency to see what possible programs they have available for students. He or she can also explain the particular curriculum needs in order to verify whether the agency is willing to provide any relevant services or resources.

Reasons for partnerships may include:
- the location of additional programs or resources to expand student learning experience,
- gaining financial support for library or school project,
- locating off campus sites where the library may hold special programs to support curricular needs,
- involving the school library media in community improvement in support of the school,
- developing a greater knowledge of concerns and issues within the community as a whole and their impact on the school.

COMPETENCY 12.0 UNDERSTAND THE RELATIONSHIP BETWEEN THE LIBRARY MEDIA PROGRAM AND INFORMATION RESOURCES BEYOND THE SCHOOL.

Skill 12.1 Recognizing the role of the library media program in connecting the school community to local, district, state, national and global resources

Students need to know the variety of information resources and agencies available to them and be given frequent opportunities to use them in order to establish good research habits. By learning about the resources available outside the school, they will more likely pursue using these services in adulthood. Here are various tips for encouraging students to utilize information resources outside of the school community:

1. Inform them of resource sharing networks that provide information. These may include public and academic libraries, Internet services, and community agencies. Some schools in districts with fully automated public library systems may provide on-line access to the public library catalog from a terminal at the school site. Public libraries also offer on-line cataloging services that can be accessed from home computers via the Internet.
2. Share informational gathering facilities with community colleges and universities.
3. Invite representatives from other information agencies to promote their programs through the schools. Post public library hours, advertisements of lectures, book reviews or other library activities. Arrange for guest speakers from Internet providers or radio and television stations. Participate in field trips to other information centers

The Board of Regents of the University System of Georgia has developed Georgia Library Learning Online, also known as GALILEO. The goal of this project was to create an online virtual library. Through GALILEO students have access to periodicals, encyclopedias, journals and government publications. Public or private libraries must provide free access to these resources for all Georgia citizens.

Skill 12.2 **Recognizing methods for establishing and maintaining connections between the school community and the larger library community (e.g., public libraries, academic libraries, special libraries, instructional support centers) for the purposes of resource sharing, networking and developing common policies and procedures**

The school library media program is no longer an isolated entity within a school. One of the most valuable activities specialists can do to promote the library media program is to develop partnerships within the community. Research has shown that strong parental and community involvement can increase student achievement.

When considering the formation of partnerships the school library media specialist must first examine the curriculum for the grade levels it serves as well as the goals for the media program. This will help to determine the people, agencies and organizations that will best help meet student needs.

To begin the process, the school library media specialist must contact the agency to see what possible programs they have available for students. He or she can also explain the particular curriculum needs in order to verify whether the agency is willing to provide any relevant services or resources.

Reasons for partnerships may include:
- the location of additional programs or resources to expand student learning experience,
- gaining financial support for library or school project,
- locating off campus sites where the library may hold special programs to support curricular needs,
- involving the school library media in community improvement in support of the school,
- developing a greater knowledge of concerns and issues within the community as a whole and their impact on the school.

Resource sharing has always been an integral part of education. Before the technology revolution, the sharing was done between teachers within schools or departments. Now it is possible to access information from around the world.

One of the most prevalent forms of resource sharing in school libraries is the use of interlibrary loans. This can mean the sharing of media resources between schools in the district or forming partnerships with the local public library. Either format provides benefits for all involved. Examples include:

1. Providing a broader information base to enable users to find and access the resources that provide the needed information.
2. Reducing or containing media center budgets.
3. Establishing cooperation with other resource providers that encourage mutual planning and standardization of control.

Skill 12.3   Demonstrating knowledge of techniques for interacting with other professionals at a variety of institutions (e.g., universities, museums, historical associations)

Collaborating with outside entities such as universities and museums expands the amount of resources available to students. It also allows each partner to maximize the use of their funding. Through collaborations with universities school library media specialists can utilize the knowledge of professors who are experts in their field. They can serve as resources for classes studying particular topics by speaking to school groups, allowing tours, or responding to student questions via email or video conferencing.

Most universities are part of a union catalog with web portals that allow patrons to search for information online and request to check out a copy of the work. In many cases the entire work or document can be viewed online as well.

Partnerships with museums and historical associations provide the unique opportunity of letting students take part in the preservation of history. Curators can create exhibits that focus on curricular topics. These exhibits can be taken to schools or students can go to the museum for special programs. Artifacts can be cataloged and placed in an online database that allows student access to resources at the point of need.

TEACHER CERTIFICATION STUDY GUIDE

Skill 12.4 Demonstrating knowledge of methods for helping members of the school community locate, access and evaluate information resources beyond the school library media center

Oftentimes, students and faculty will need to complete research that is beyond the scope of their institution's size and ability. However, the library media specialist can still assist in this research process through resource sharing.

Resource sharing systems include:

1. **Interlibrary loan**. The advent of computer databases has simplified the process of locating sources in other libraries. Local public library collections can be accessed from terminals in the media center. Physical access depends on going to the branch where the material is housed.
2. **Networking systems**. Sharing information has become even easier with the use of network services. Files can be shared and accessed from room to room, school to school and city to city. Resources can be shared within a small geographic location such as a school by the use of a local area network, or LAN. A wide area network, or WAN, is used to communicate over a larger area such as a school district or city.
    a. E-mail allows educators to communicate across the state.
    b. On-line services (i.e., Internet providers) offer access to a specific menu of locations. Monthly fees and time charges must be budgeted.
    c. Individual city or county network systems. These are community sponsored networks, often part of the public library system, which provide Internet access for the price of a local phone call. A time limit usually confines an individual search to allow more users access.
    d. On-line continuing education programs offer courses and degrees through at-home study. Large school districts provide lessons for homebound students or home school advocates.
    e. Bulletin boards allow individuals or groups to converse electronically with persons in another place.
3. **Telecommunications**. Using telephone and television as the media for communication, telecommunications is used primarily for distance learning. Many universities or networks of universities provide workshops, conferences and college credit courses for educators. They also offer courses for senior high school students in subjects that could not generate adequate class counts in their home schools. Large school districts offer broadcast programming for homebound or home schooled students. The advantage of telecommunication programming (as opposed to networking systems) is that students are provided with a phone number so they can interact with the instructors or information providers.

Skill 12.5 Recognizing the role of professional associations and journals in maintaining current, research-based knowledge about information resources and technologies

Professional development allows the school library media specialist to stay abreast of current trends in school library media programs. The media specialist should be actively involved in the following national, state and local Library Media Organizations.

National:
American Library Association (ALA)
American Association of School Library (AASL)
International Reading Association (IRA)
Association for Supervision and Curriculum Development (ASCD)
National Staff Development Council (NSCD)

State:
Georgia Association for Instructional Technology (GAIT)
Georgia Library Media Association (GLMA)
Georgia Association of Educational Technology Professionals (GAETP)
Georgia Library Association (GLA)
Georgia Educational Technology Conference (GaETC)

The media specialist should attend national, state, and regional conferences annually such as:

- Technology Education Conferences
- National Educational Computing Conferences

The media specialist should subscribe to at least three library or education-related publications. Here is a list of professional journals that are relevant to media specialists.

- *The Library Quarterly*
    - Scholarly research regarding all areas of librarianship.
- *School Library Media Research*
    - Published by American Association of School Librarians.
    - The successor to *School Library Media Quarterly Online*.
    - Dedicated to providing research concerning the management, implementation and evaluation of school library media programs.
- *Library Trends*
    - Explores critical trends in professional librarianship.
    - Includes practical applications and literature reviews.
- *American Libraries*
    - Published by the American Library Association.
    - Provides the latest news and updates from the association.

- *School Library Journal*
    - Serves school and public librarians who work with the young.
    - Provides information needed to integrate libraries into all aspects of the school curriculum.
    - Provides resources to become effective technology leaders.
    - Provides resources to assist with collection development

In addition to subscriptions to several of these journals, the media specialist should also participate in discussion forums such as LM_NET. These forums will help the special attain advice unique for the situation for the specialist's media center.

SUBAREA IV. LIBRARY MEDIA PROGRAM ADMINISTRATION

COMPETENCY 13.0 UNDERSTAND PRINCIPLES AND PRACTICES FOR MANAGING LIBRARY MEDIA INFORMATION RESOURCES

Skill 13.1 Demonstrating knowledge of strategies for selecting, analyzing and evaluating library media collections (e.g., print, nonprint, electronic) to develop a collection that supports the needs of a diverse population

A collection of resources that closely ties the school's instructional program as well as the developmental and cultural needs of students is crucial to the school library media program.

To ensure the collection meets student needs there are steps the media specialist can take:

1. Stay abreast of changes in curriculum as well as the types of resources needed to meet those needs.
2. Work closely with teachers to determine resources needed.
3. Work closely with staff to determine policies and procedures.
4. Develop specific processes for evaluating and updating the collection.
5. Have access to up-to-date collection monitoring and evaluation tools and reviewing resources.
6. Support the circulation of resources by sharing information with teachers and allowing them to preview new resources as well as take part in the selection process.

Each school library media center should develop a policy tailored to the philosophy and objectives of that school's educational program. This policy provides guidelines by which all participants in the selection process can get insight into their responsibilities. The policy statement should reflect the following factors.

1. Compatibility with district, state, regional and national guidelines (see Skill 1.2).
2. Adherence to the principles of intellectual freedom and the specifics of copyright law.
3. Recognition of the rights of individuals or groups to challenge policies, procedures or selected items, and the establishment of procedures for dealing fairly with such challenges.
4. Recognition of users needs and interests, including community demographics.

The policy should include the school library media center's mission and the criteria used in the selection process. General criteria for the selection of all media include:

1. **Authenticity**. Media should be accurate, current and authoritative. Copyright or printing dates are indicators of currency, but examination of content is often necessary to determine the relevance of the subject matter to its intended use. Research into the reputations of contributors and comparison to other materials by the same producer will provide insight into its literary quality.
2. **Appropriateness of Subject Matter**. Consider suitability to the school's educational objectives, scope of coverage, treatment and arrangement of content, importance of content to the user, and appropriateness to users' ability levels and learning styles.
3. **Appeal.** Consideration of the artistic quality and language appropriateness will help in the selection of media that students will enjoy using. Properly selected materials should stimulate creativity and inspire further learning.

As the specialist continually evaluates the items in the collection, he or she should also focus on these various elements of a collection development plan:

1. Knowledge of the existing collection or the ability to create a new collection.
2. Knowledge of the external environment of the media center, including the school and the community.
3. Assessment of school programs and user needs.
4. Development of overall policies and procedures.
5. Guidelines for specific selection decisions.
6. Evaluation criteria.
7. Establishment of a process for planning and implementing the collection plan.
8. Establishment of acquisition policies and procedures.
9. Establishment of maintenance program.
10. Establishment of procedures for evaluating the collection.

After recognizing these elements, the specialist should follow the following procedures for implementing the plan:

1. Learn the collection. A library media specialist, new to a school with an existing collection, should use several approaches to becoming familiar with the collection.
    a. Browse the shelves. Note your degree of familiarity with titles. Examine items that are unfamiliar to you. Determine the relationship between the materials on similar subjects in different formats. Include the reference and professional collections in your browse. Consider the accessibility of various media and the ease with which they can be located by users.
    b. Locate the center's procedures manual. Determine explanations for any seeming irregularities in the collection.
    c. Determine if any portions of the collection are housed in areas outside the media center.

    If the library media specialist is required to create a new collection, he or she should
    a. Consult with the district director about new school collection policies.
    b. Examine the collections of other comparable schools.
    c. Examine companies, like Baker and Taylor's, who establishes new collections based on criteria provided by the school.

2. Learn about the community.
    a. Examine the relationship of the media center to the total school program and other information agencies.
    b. Become familiar with the school, cultural, economic and political characteristics of the community and their influence on the schools.

3. Study the school's curriculum and the needs of the users (students and faculty). Examine the proportions of basic skills to enrichment offerings, academic or vocational courses, and requirements and electives.
    a. Determine the ability levels and grouping techniques for learners.
    b. Determine instructional objectives of teachers in various content areas or grade levels.
4. Examine existing policies and procedures for correlation to data acquired in researching the school and community.
5. Examine specific selection procedures to determine if guidelines are best met.
6. Examine evaluation criteria for effectiveness in maintaining an appropriate collection.
7. Examine the process to determine that accurate procedures are in place to meet the criteria.

8. Examine the acquisition plan. Determine the procedure by which materials are ordered, received, paid for and processed.
9. Examine maintenance procedures for repairing or replacing materials and equipment, replacing consumables, and discarding non-repairable items.
10. Examine the policies and procedures for evaluation, then examine the collection itself to determine if policies and procedures are contributing to quality and quantity.

Procedures for maintaining the collection are perhaps the most important in the collection plan. The plan itself must provide efficient, economical procedures for keeping materials and equipment in usable condition.

Maintenance policies for equipment and some policies for materials are determined at the district level. Procedures to satisfy these policies are followed at the building level.

1. Replacement or discard of damaged items based on comparison of repair to replacement cost. Districts usually maintain repair contracts with external contractors for major repairs that cannot be done at the school or district media service center.
2. Equipment inventory and records on repair or disposal. Usage records help with the transfer of usable items from school to school

Skill 13.2   Identifying strategies for involving the learning community in the evaluation, selection and deselection of library media information resources

A collection that is current and meets the needs of staff and students often requires the specialist to re-evaluate and discard worn or outdated materials. There are many resources that provide assistance with procedures for weeding out these materials. A few items for the specialist to take into consideration when reviewing and weeding out the collection are:

1. Weeding should be an ongoing process.
2. Criteria for weeding is sometimes subjective, but can be based on the following categories:

   USE – look for materials not circulated regularly
   WEAR – torn, stained or ripped materials may be repaired let go
   SUBJECT – the information in the resource is outdated, no longer valid or has been replaced by a newer, updated version of the material
   AVAILABLE ELSEWHERE – if the material is readily available electronically or through another resource and is not often used, it may be worth discarding

A popular acronym to consider when weeding is MUSTIE.

- **M**isleading
- **U**gly
- **S**uperseded
- **T**rivial
- **I**rrelevant
- **E**lsewhere

When weeding, consider extenuating circumstances that might warrant the saving of materials, such as works by local authors, memorial gifts or local histories.

Here are the suggested weeding procedures for each Dewey level:

- 000 – encyclopedias every five years, other materials no more than eight years
- 100 – five to eight years
- 200 – can be high turnover with religious books – keep current
- 300 – replace almanacs every two years, keep political information current
- 400 – check for wear and tear frequently
- 500 – continuously update to make sure scientific information is current
- 600 – continuously update medical information as older information can be misleading or dangerous
- 700 – keep until worn
- 800 – keep until worn
- 900 – weed about every two years
- Biography – keep most current or best written titles
- Adult fiction – weed for multiple copies, keep those in best shape and that have the most literary value
- Young-adult and children's fiction – same as adult fiction
- Reference – weed for currency and accuracy

See also Skill 13.1

Skill 13.3 **Identifying and applying standard procedures for classifying and cataloging library media information resources (e.g., Dewey Decimal System, US MARC, Sears)**

Two classification systems are prevalent in the United States.

1. The Library of Congress System Heading uses a system which has been adopted by many colleges and universities since the 1960's. This is usually comprised of five large red volumes that are housed in the reference section.
2. The Dewey Decimal System is used predominately in schools and public libraries.

The purpose of both systems is to provide universal standards of organizing collections. These systems facilitate location of materials within a collection and enable institutions to share information and materials that are uniformly grouped.

The MARC format is relatively universal and enables a school library to utilize many commercial automation tools. The format allows for unlimited fields which provide more efficient cataloging for both print and non-print items. Each field is marked with a tag that represents a specific piece of information (i.e., 245 tag lists title information and the 520 tag marks the summary).

The MARC format assists in preserving bibliographic integrity. Bibliographic integrity refers to the accuracy and uniformity with which items are catalogued. A standard set of international rules called the *Anglo-American Cataloguing Rules*, enables users to locate materials equally well in all libraries that subscribe to these rules. To maintain this integrity, catalogers should complete the following:

1. Recognize an International Standard Bibliographic Description (ISBD) that establishes the order in which bibliographic elements will appear in catalog entries.
2. Note changes that occur after each five years review of ISBD.
3. Agree to catalog all materials using the AACR standards.

Here are the components of a basic bibliographic record that may be used in LCC or DDC shelflist cards or in OCLC's MARC records for automated systems:

1. **Call Number**. Includes DDC or LCCN classification number followed by a book identification identifier (numerals or letters).
2. **Author Main Entry Heading**. Use name by which author is most commonly known even if that name is a pseudonym.
3. **Title and Statement of Responsibility Area**. Include title, subtitle or parallel titles and name(s) of authors, editors, illustrators, translators or groups functioning in authorship capacity.
4. **Edition Statement**. Provide ordinal number of edition.

5. **Material Specific Details**. Used with only four materials (computer files, cartographic materials, printed music, and serials in all formats).
6. **Area of Publication, Distribution, etc.** Include place of publication, name of publisher and copyright date.
7. **Physical Description Area.** Include the extent of the work (number of pages, volumes or other units); illustrative matter; size/dimensions; and accompanying materials.
8. **Series**. Provide title of series and publication information if different from statement of responsibility.
9. **Notes**. Provide information to clarify any other descriptive components, including audio-visual formats or reading levels.
10. **Standard numbers**. Provide ISBN, ISSN, or LCC number, price or other terms of availability.

It is necessary for all entries to have standardized subject headings. *Sear's List of Subject Headings* is generally used in Dewey Decimal classification while the Library of Congress has its own subject heading list.

Skill 13.4   Identifying practices and policies (e.g., regarding cataloging, circulation, collection development, scheduling) that ensure flexible and equitable access to facilities and resources based on users' needs

Circulation policies and procedures should be flexible to allow ready access and secure to protect borrowers' rights of confidentiality.

The components of circulation procedures include:
1. Circulation system. Whether manual or automated, this system should
   a. be simple to use for convenience of staff and the efficiency of borrowing,
   b. provide for the loan and retrieval of print and non-print materials and equipment,
   c. and facilitate the collection of circulation statistics.
2. Rules governing circulation.
   a. Length of loan period.
   b. Process for handling overdues.
   c. Limitations.
      i. Number of items circulable to individual borrower.
      ii. Overnight loan for special items (vertical file materials, reference books, audio-visual materials or equipment).
      iii. Reserve collections.
3. Rules governing fines for damages or lost materials.
4. Security provisions.
   a. Theft detection devices on print and non-print media.
   b. Straps or lock-downs on equipment transported by cart.

Skill 13.5 **Demonstrating knowledge of the role of technology in the organization, management and circulation of resources**

There are three main categories that must be considered when preparing to convert to an automated library management system. These categories include the budget, the technical considerations and the data needing conversion.

The options available during the conversion process are often determined by the funds available. Necessary purchases would include the software, a barcode scanner for checkout, necessary hardware upgrades, and technical support. Other options could include a web based searching option for home use and payment to other companies for the conversion of records.

Before beginning the process of conversion, have a well-defined plan and take small steps as time and money allow.

Technical considerations fall into the software, hardware and infrastructure categories. When selecting software for library management, check local or state recommendations before making any decisions. The platform should match the computer systems most prevalent in your district. If your school is predominantly MAC based then use a MAC platform; if Windows, use Windows. Before purchasing the software, make sure the computers in the school will support the requirements of the software and that the network infrastructure is in place to provide maximum access. District technical support staff should be able to assist with these decisions. It will be important to purchase or make sure that technical support is provided for the automation software manufacturer. This may involve an extra expense, but will be money well spent especially during the initial setup phase.

After the technical requirements are in place, it is time to begin the data conversion process. Transferring the current card catalog into electronic format can be a daunting job. It helps first to thoroughly weed the collection. By weeding, time is saved by not converting titles that will be discarded.

The actual conversion of information to electronic format will be the most time consuming task. Options include inputting the data onsite or hiring a company to convert the shelflist to electronic format. Budget is generally the biggest consideration. If the choice is to convert onsite a wise investment would be the purchase of MARC CD-ROMS. This will make the process move much faster. There are companies who will convert the shelflist to MARC format for a rather minimal charge considering the time it takes to enter everything by hand. Explore the possibilities of utilizing such services and determine the impact on the automation budget.

Once the shelflist has been converted to electronic format, books must be barcoded. This generally involves printing barcode stickers and placing them on each and every book. Volunteers and student helpers can make this process move quickly.

Next, all patrons need to be added into the system. This can often be conducted by importing data from the school's attendance management system. If not, information will need to be keyed in by hand.

Once all of the information is in then the school library media specialist needs to set up basic information such as checkout limits, the amount of time a book can be checked out, and other basic housekeeping information.

The conversion to an automated system is a lot of work, but the benefits far outweigh the time it would take to complete the process.

COMPETENCY 14.0   **UNDERSTAND PRINCIPLES AND PRACTICES RELATED TO THE MANAGEMENT OF TECHNOLOGICAL RESOURCES OF THE LIBRARY MEDIA PROGRAM.**

Skill 14.1   **Recognizing and comparing the advantages and limitations of various technological resources, formats and services**

With the flood of technological advances in the past few decades school library media centers have a wealth of non-print information available. Examples include:

- **Computerized databases** like online dictionaries, encyclopedias and information databases can be easily accessed. These databases are easily searched using keywords and generally contain cross-references to similar information. The speed of computerized databases dramatically reduces time searching for information.
- **Online catalogs** include catalogs of information similar to a database or catalogs for ordering resources. The information can be located using keyword searches that allow the user to drill down for more information.
- **CD-ROMs** are compact discs that contain software and other multi-media resources. The resources can include electronic atlases, encyclopedias, and simulations. Like the online encyclopedias, the storage capacity of CDs allows for relevant video and audio to be included with the articles. Interactive resources such as simulations can also be incorporated in these resources.
- **Video** can be found in a wide variety of formats. Videotapes in various formats are still part of the resources found in many school library media centers. Upgrading equipment and formats can be costly, so school budgets may still require use of older formats such as VHS. Many video cameras used in schools utilize smaller types of tapes such as Hi 8 or Mini DVD cassettes for recording. Video can also be found on DVDs. As technology changes and the format for videos improve, schools will eventually move to newer formats as they arise.

When equipment and formats become an issue, schools can turn to online videos to supplement their collection. A variety of educational videos can be found online. Companies such as United Streaming focus on providing quality educational videos. The main issue with viewing videos online is the bandwidth these resources require. Bandwidth is the amount of information that can be sent over a network. When a file such as a video takes up a large part of the bandwidth, other resources begin to slow down. There are various formats of video, and some require more space than others.

Video file extensions can include:
.avi – Audio Video Interactive file
.mpeg – MPEG Video Files
.rm – Real Media File
.qt – QuickTime Movie
.wmv – Windows Media Video File

Because of bandwidth concerns, careful consideration and consultation with the network administrator needs to take place before the use of viewing videos online becomes widespread.

- **Audio** can also be found in a variety of formats within schools. The issue for using older formats involves the cost to upgrade equipment. Cassette tapes contain both music and audio versions of books. As cassettes become worn or damaged they are being replaced by CDs. Audio clips can be found online, and these are often called podcasts. Podcasts are audio files found online, many of which are in the format of a radio broadcast. As with video, the use of streaming audio from the Internet does cut into a network's bandwidth. However, audio files are not usually as large.

Skill 14.2   Applying knowledge of criteria for selecting and managing existing and emerging technological applications, materials, services and formats to support and enhance the curriculum

In addition to the general selection criteria, certain other specific criteria must be imposed when selecting media and equipment. Types of media include:

1. Printed or display media (pamphlets, handouts, flannel boards, flip charts etc.).
2. Overhead transparencies.
3. Slides and filmstrips.
4. Audiotape recordings.
5. Videotape recordings.
6. Computer software.
7. CD-ROM and laser disks.

Some or all criteria may be applied to the media formats:

1. **Technical quality**. The sound quality, picture focus, font size, screen color, and physical dimensions must be technically correct and artistically appealing for the information within to be appreciated and absorbed by the learner.
2. **Packaging**. Non-print media need to be packaged in reusable containers if they are to be circulated and protected from wear and tear.

TEACHER CERTIFICATION STUDY GUIDE

3. **Cost**. The advantages of one format over another must be studied for the limits of the current budget, the size of the group to be served, and the durability of the product in terms of the investment. Some products may be considered for rental rather than purchase.
4. **Applicability**. The product should be suitable for available equipment to use it with, appropriate to the climate and environment in which it will be used, and potentially usable with individuals as well as small or large groups.
5. **Educational value**. If possible, the product advertisement should provide evidence that the selected media format has been tested with learners to prove its value to the learning process.

Besides the criteria for evaluating formats, a media specialist should also evaluate possible equipment with the following criteria in mind:

1. **Balance**. The amount of audio-visual materials, the frequency of need for these materials, and the preference of teachers will influence the number of items to purchase. District guidelines may set minimum levels.
2. **Condition**. Some years the budget may need to take into consideration the need for replacing worn or damaged pieces of equipment in the collection. Some new equipment is essential to keep up with new media formats.

When looking to add, replace or repair equipment, remember these resources:

1. Company catalogs.
2. State or district approved lists.
3. Services for free or reduced cost products: ITV, MECC.
4. Preview or observation of products.

Skill 14.3 **Demonstrating knowledge of strategies for providing support and training to the learning community in the use of technological resources**

Because we are in the business of teaching, all technologies must be viewed as educational tools. To enable teachers to understand the way these technologies can be applied in their classrooms, they must understand the relationship between these tools and learning needs. The school library media professionals must be able to update teachers on this correlation.

1. Conduct timely, short in-service activities to demonstrate and allow teachers to manipulate new technologies and plan classroom uses
2. Clip articles or write reviews to distribute to teachers with suggestions for application in their particular learning environment.
3. Offer to plan and teach lessons in different content areas.

For more information on how to plan and implement in service training sessions, please refer to Skill 10.3.

Skill 14.4 Applying knowledge of strategies for coordinating the use of technological resources with administrators, faculty and staff

In a perfect world all students and teachers would have access to all of the technological resources that they needed exactly when they needed it. In reality, resources must be shared and the media specialist often has the role of coordinating their use.

The mission of the school library media center is to provide physical and intellectual access to information at the point of need. This is best accomplished through open and flexibly scheduled classes. A flexible schedule promotes learning at the point of need and provides the media specialist with opportunities to work collaboratively with both staff and students.

The issue of flexible access is especially distressing to elementary school library media specialists who are placed in the "related arts wheel," providing planning time for art, music, and physical education teachers. "Closed" or rigid scheduling (i.e., scheduling classes to meet regularly for instruction in the library) prohibits the implementation of the integrated program philosophy essential to the principles of intellectual freedom.

The AASL Position Statement on Flexible Scheduling asserts that schools must adopt a philosophy of full integration of library media into the total educational program. This integration assures a partnership of students, teachers and school library media specialists in the use of readily accessible materials and services when they are appropriate to the classroom curriculum.

All parties in the school community, including teachers, school administrators, district administrators and school board members, must share the responsibility for contributing to flexible access.

Research on the validity of flexible access reinforces the need for cooperative planning with teachers, an objective that cannot be met if the school library media specialist has no time for the required planning sessions. Rigid scheduling denies students the freedom to come to the library during the school day for pleasurable reading and self-motivated inquiry activities vital to the development of critical thinking, problem solving and exploratory skills. Without flexible access, the library becomes just another self-contained classroom.

COMPETENCY 15.0   **UNDERSTAND PRINCIPLES AND PRACTICES RELATED TO THE MANAGEMENT OF HUMAN, FINANCIAL AND PHYSICAL RESOURCES OF THE LIBRARY MEDIA PROGRAM.**

Skill 15.1   **Recognizing methods of developing and evaluating policies and procedures that support the mission of the school and address the specific needs of the library media program (e.g., collection development and maintenance, challenged materials, acceptable use policies)**

Every member of the school community has a different perspective on the learning environment. Because of this, it is always preferable to develop and evaluate local policies and procedures with the aid of a library advisory committee. Here are the various perspectives that community members can bring to the committee meetings.

Participants	Role
Administrator	clarifies school vision and goals.
Media specialist	identifies factors such as time, personnel, resources and budget that affect school goals.
Teacher	identifies media center resources and services that correlate with instruction.
Student	identifies materials and activities that fulfill learning needs.
Parents (Optional)	identify avenues of communication with parents and community.

The library media specialist should be prepared to discuss how the goals and objectives of the media center coincide with those for the school and the learning community. For more information on how to develop objectives for the media center, please see Skill 11.4. For more information on how to evaluate the current state of the media center in order to create new goals, please see Skill 13.1.

Skill 15.2 Identifying strategies for communicating the status and needs of the library media program to the larger learning community and for advocating for ongoing administrative support for the library media program

Establish and nurture an administrative partnership with the principal and district director of media to develop, establish and fund library program goals. In larger districts that have a district director of media, avenues of support may be clearly defined. In smaller districts, where the media director also handles other administrative duties or where there is no district coordinator, support is based on the lobbying efforts of the school library media specialist. In any case, the principal must be the media center's staunchest ally. Present the annual program goals and implementation procedures to the principal early in the school year for his or her input and approval. Invite the principal to participate in faculty in services and advisory committee meetings. Ask to be included on the school's curriculum planning team.

By doing so, you will exhibit your willingness to assume a leadership role in integrating the library media program into the total school program. Make every attempt to ensure that some phase of the library media program appears in each year's school improvement plan.

Within your district, work with the district media director and other school library media specialists to establish and maintain a uniformly excellent district library media program. Continually evaluate the goals and objectives of the school program compared to the district program and matched to the users' needs as identified in annual assessments. Keep apprised of state certification requirements for certificate renewal and complete renewal requirements in a timely manner.

As a means to provide outreach to the extended learning community, attend school board meetings. Be aware of all issues affecting the media program, instruction and the budget. Invite county or area superintendents and school board members to district media meetings to discuss issues and plan improvements. Make yourself and your enthusiasm for the library media program visible.

A knowledgeable library media specialist is the best human resource in the school. There is perhaps no better promotion for the media center than having students, teachers and administrators seeking information from the library media center staff.

Systematically assess program needs on an annual basis. Always have available statistics about media center use, lesson plans or visitation schedules, and written evaluations of instructional activities. Make presentations to School Improvement Committees, parent support groups or community agencies.

Making thorough, accurate reports indicates a well-managed program and encourages maximum support.

By reaching outside of the learning community, you will help solidify the public's perception of a library media center as a crucial part of any lifelong learning environment. Attend college courses, in service training and professional conferences. Offer to teach night college courses, supervise a library media candidate, offer workshops for school faculty and make presentations at conferences. But, remember to be selective. Never forsake your ethical responsibility to serve patrons by overextending your commitments.

Skill 15.3 Demonstrating knowledge of accepted management principles and practices for the selection, supervision, training and evaluation of library media staff and volunteers

The school library media specialist has many responsibilities, from developing program goals, collections, and budgets to consulting with teachers and students. Because of all these responsibilities, the media specialist often leads several paraprofessional and nonprofessional staff members.

The paraprofessional is a person qualified for a special area of media such as graphics, photography, instructional television, electronics, media production or computer technology. Often called a technical assistant, this person has training in his or her specialty and often holds an associate's or bachelor's degree in this specialty. While the paraprofessional may have some education training, he or she will most likely not have a bachelor's degree in library or information sciences, although some community colleges are now offering certificates in Library Assistantship.

The paraprofessional's responsibilities are in the areas of production, maintenance, and special services to students and teachers. Some of his duties might include:

1. Working with teachers in the design and production of media for classroom instruction.
2. Creating promotional materials and preparing special need media (e.g., video yearbook, audio or videotape duplication, materials for faculty meetings and staff development activities).
3. Operating and maintaining production equipment (e.g., laminator, Thermofax).
4. Maintaining computers and peripherals.
5. Evaluating media and equipment collection and recommending purchases.
6. Developing ways to use existing and emerging technologies.
7. Assisting teachers and students in locating and using media and equipment.

8. Repairing or making provisions for repair of materials and equipment.
9. Circulating equipment.
10. Maintaining records on circulation, maintenance and repair of media and equipment.

The non-professional staff assumes responsibility for operational procedures (i.e., clerical, secretarial, technical, maintenance) that relieve the school library professional and paraprofessional of routine tasks so they can better perform their responsibilities.

Some specific nonprofessional activities include:

1. Conducting accounting and bookkeeping procedures.
2. Unpacking, processing and shelving new materials.
3. Processing correspondences, records, manuals, etc.
4. Circulating materials and equipment.
5. Assisting with materials production.
6. Assisting with maintenance and repair of materials and equipment.
7. Handling accounting procedures.
8. Assisting with inventory.
9. Assisting with services provided by electronic and computer equipment.

When considering nonprofessional and paraprofessional staff, remember that all staffing plans need to be based upon certification and accreditation guidelines. The number of students at a school can determine staffing numbers and positions as well as the increase of technology. While it is always important to have adequate technical support and media staff, resources are not infinite, and the library media specialist must examine and evaluate the responsibilities of current staff members in order to identify whether additional assistance is necessary. One method would be to have each staff member complete a time analysis for a week or so. This allows the specialist to compare the results from this to the actual job description, using his or her findings to identify staffing needs within the media program. Outside evaluators can also be effective in determining needs.

The diversity of user needs, school enrollments and school/district support services are some factors that affect staff size. Oftentimes, the duties of staff members at different levels can overlap, only differing in the amount of decision-making and accountability.

In addition to staff members, volunteers can also help with circulation and supplemental tasks that reflect their unique talents and experiences, but they should never be used as substitutes for paid clerical and technical staff. Student assistants, like volunteers, may be trained to assist the media specialist but should not be given duties that are the responsibilities of paid nonprofessionals. Students might assist with production of materials, maintenance of the decoration and physical appearance of the center, instruction in materials location, use of electronic/computer databases, and shelving books and periodicals. It is recommended that student aides be given course credit or certificates of achievement to reward them for their services.

When working with nonprofessional staff, volunteers, and student assistants, realize that those who are not trained as support staff will need to be trained on the job. Here are several strategies for training these individuals:

1. Using the district's job description and evaluation instrument for the particular position, prioritizing skills and responsibilities in order from greatest to least immediacy.
2. Determining the individual's knowledge and mastery of skills by observing performance.
3. Planning a systematic training of remaining skills to be addressed one at a time.

The supervision of media professionals is the responsibility of an administrator, and the supervision of support staff is the responsibility of the head library media specialist (if that position is administrative) or of an administrator who receives input from the media specialist. Periodic oral evaluations and annual written evaluations using the appropriate instrument should be conducted for each media staff member. These evaluations should result in suggestions for training or personal development.

Skill 15.4   Identifying types, characteristics and uses of financial budgets and reports and demonstrating basic knowledge of funding sources for library media programs

In preparation for constructing the budget for the school library media center, the school media professionals need to consider the following items:

1. The standards set by state departments of education, local school boards and regional accreditation associations. Changes in standards may necessitate changes in local budget planning.
2. The sources of funds that support the media center program.
3. The prioritized list of program goals and the cost of meeting these goals.

Determining the relationship between program goals and funding involve the study of

1. past inventories and projections of future needs,
2. quantitative and qualitative collection standards at all levels,
3. school and district curriculum plans,
4. community needs
5. fiscal deadlines.

AASL/AECT guidelines provide for four factors in calculating the budget for the print and non-print collection: variation in student population, attrition by weeding, attrition by date and attrition by loss. A formula for an estimated budget is then calculated based on points established for each of these factors. The estimation for replacement is figured on a base number of collection items required regardless of school size. The minimum collection standard is determined by the state or regional accreditation requirements.

Another method of estimating a budget for the print collection is based on the types of materials needed: replacement books, periodicals, books for growth and expansion, and reference books. It is recommended that 5% of the total books in the print collection be used in the formula.

In districts in which the school library media center allocation is not calculated on local recommendations but on an across the board per capita figure, the school library media specialist must then work with the administration to secure necessary funds from the school budget. If funds are not categorized at the district level, the school library media specialist must then set a percentage for each category based on the previously discussed factors.

Having considered all factors, the budget process should parallel budget plans to the program goals and objectives. To achieve this correlation the process should follow these steps:

1. Communicate program and budget considerations to administration, faculty, student body and community groups, allowing sufficient time for input from all groups.
2. Work with representatives from all groups to finalize short-range objectives and review long-range goals for use of funds.
3. Build a system of flexible encumbrance and transferal of funds as changes in need occur.
4. As part of the program promotion, communicate budgetary concerns to all interested parties.

Skill 15.5 Demonstrating knowledge of issues related to running a library media program within a budget

Unlike public libraries, school library media centers are not usually the recipients of endowments or private gifts. Instead, school library media centers receive money from local and state tax dollars. The major portion of the funds comes from district allotments for instructional materials or capital outlay that are regulated by the state. Schools that have accreditation must adhere to regional guidelines that assure the accreditation. The funding formulas specifically used for school library media budgets vary from district to district but basically comply with the following regulations.

Federal:

1. Block grants included in federal education acts. Awarded to states or specific districts, these grants are limited in scope and time. They must be applied for on a competitive basis and renewal depends on the recipient's ability to prove that grant objectives have been met.

2. Current federal funds are earmarked for innovative technologies, not operating costs.

State:

1. Local operation. School library media center funds are generally allocated from the district operating budget. The funds may be administered at the district or school level according to a per capita figure that is adequate to meet operation costs and contractual obligations. Many media centers host book fairs to supplement inadequate budgets.

2. Regional guidelines. SAC produces an expenditures requirement based on student body size, allowing a school to average expenditures over a three-year period in which averaged expenditures do not fall below the standard.

3. State funds provided by special legislation. Most special funds have been in the form of block grants. Block grants are funds earmarked for a specific purpose. Schools generally must apply for such funds. One example is the technology block grants that have appeared in recent years. These grants have provided funds for retrofitting schools to create local area networks, wide-area networks and telecommunications services.

In addition to official funding sources, there are other forms of assistance from the community that should be reflected in the budget plan. Because this assistance is in the form of service rather than real dollars, estimated values must be determined. Some community assistance includes:

1. Partnerships with local businesses. Free wiring from cable television companies, guest speakers, distance learning opportunities and workshops in new technologies are just a few possible services.

2. Education support groups. The education committee of the local chamber of commerce, a private education economic council or parent associations may conduct fund-raisers or offer mini-grants.

3. Corporate grants. Many large companies provide grants for specific topics such as technology, science, math and reading. The grant may involve providing equipment or funds to be used for a specific purpose.

COMPETENCY 16.0 UNDERSTAND THE COMPREHENSIVE AND COLLABORATIVE NATURE OF STRATEGIC PLANNING AND ASSESSMENT FOR THE LIBRARY MEDIA PROGRAM.

Skill 16.1 Demonstrating knowledge of strategies for collaborating with teachers, administrators, students and others in the learning community to develop, implement and assess long term strategic plans for the library media program

Once an initial program evaluation has been completed, program goals and objectives may be determined. These goals and objectives help to break down the overall vision into areas that the school feels are most important for the successful operation of a school library media program. Some of these goals may already be determined by national or state guidelines that districts administrators have agreed to maintain. Sometimes, a district operates without a program to guide school library media centers. In that case each school must be responsible not only for setting its own criteria but also for inspiring some district planning.

The first step would be to define major goals. A goal is a broad statement of an intended outcome that reflects the mission of the school library media program that provides direction.

A goal is a long-range plan. Therefore, when planning a school library media program based on an assessment of school and student characteristics, the program planning team should factor in these elements.

A long-range plan should

1. Extend from 3-5 years.
2. Incorporate the goals of the other departments (grade levels or content teams) in the school.
3. Be stated in terms that are non-limiting. The goal should be an achievable aim, not a pipe dream.

Specific goals for school library media centers are outlined in *Information Power: Building Partnerships for Learning.* Key points include:

- providing access to resources and information through integrated activities on a variety of levels
- providing physical access to a wide variety of resources and information from various locations including outside agencies and electronic resources
- assist patrons in locating and evaluating information
- collaborate with teachers and others
- facilitate the lifelong learning process

- build a school library media program that acts as the hub of all learning within the school
- provide resources that embrace differences culturally and socially and support concepts of intellectual freedom

Skill 16.2   Identifying strategies for aligning the resources and services of the library media program with information literacy standards and with the school's goals, objectives and standards

At the school level, it is important for the media specialist to work closely with classroom teachers during grade level planning meetings to plan, design, teach and evaluate various instructional activities. They should serve on curriculum development committees both at the school and district level to assist with the integration of information literacy skills and provide resources. By serving on these committees and collaborating with staff the media specialist is best able to determine the resources and services that meet the needs of the school's curriculum.

In addition to the media specialist's involvement within the learning community, there are other resources and opportunities at the district and state level. An example of this is the ongoing collaboration between the Georgia Library Media Association and the Georgia Department of Education. These two groups have worked diligently to align services and standards pertaining to school library media programs. Since 1998 these two entities have pulled together media specialists from across the state to attend the yearly Leadership Institute. The institute's original task focused on the aligning of objectives and it has grown to creating tools that help both teachers and media specialists better integrate information skills.

Skill 16.3   Recognizing methods for evaluating the effectiveness of policies, procedures and operations of a library media program and for modifying the library media program based on evaluation results

A policy is the written statement of principle in which the policy-making agency guarantees a management practice or course of action that is expedient and consistent. A procedure is the course of action taken to execute the policy. In government, legislation is policy and law enforcement is procedure.

Educational policy makers include Congress and state legislatures, state and local school boards, national library media organizations and school library media program managers. Policies adopted at the local level must support both district school board policies and state laws. Regulations concerning certification, state budget allocations and standards for selecting and approving state-adopted instructional materials are developed at the state level.

Matters such as collection development and responding to challenges of materials are usually set at district level. Local issues such as hours of operation, circulation of materials and equipment, and personnel supervision are set by the appropriate school policy makers for library media.

Procedures for administering district and state policies are usually determined by usual practice or local precedence. Procedures for specific administration tasks such as determining budget categories, expending funds, maintaining collection size should be clearly stated in a school library media procedures manual.

The two basic sources for district policies are school board rules and the procedures manual from district media services offices. Information provided in these documents should be reviewed before any school level planning is done.

It is also necessary to know which policies and procedures are the responsibility of the district and which ones are the responsibilities of the school. For example, school boards are charged with the responsibility to set propriety standards for selection of instructional materials. However, school boards do not select the texts or library books for individual schools. Procedures for implementing propriety standards are determined at each school site based on the needs of its students.

School boards may set policy for a challenge and identify a procedure for its sequential investigation. As a defender of intellectual freedom and a trained educator, the school library media specialist should have the latitude to recommend and purchase quality materials. She should also be prepared to substantiate those purchases in terms of readability, social appropriateness, and artistic quality.

Operational procedures also change from district-to-district. Some counties have centralized reprographics facilities; therefore, district policies are set for reproduction of materials that comply with copyright laws and district procedures for formatting, according to the type of equipment used, are spelled out in a printed manual which should be available at all school sites.
Some counties have centralized materials processing so that classification and cataloging procedures are administered at the county level.

It is always preferable to develop local policies and procedures with the aid of a library advisory committee. Once the advisory committee has formulated acceptable policies and procedures, the district director and/or directors of elementary and secondary instruction should review and provide input before adoption.

In terms of staffing, school districts are bound by law to maintain a properly certified staff, but it is the obligation of the employee to learn about professional development activities, to take six course credits within the five-year period, and to submit proof of these activities to the certification officer prior to the June 30 deadline in the renewal year.

The most efficient method of communicating policies and procedures to the faculty is the library media procedures manual. This manual should first present the mission and long-range objectives and then the specific policies designed to meet these objectives. Specific procedures for using the resources and services should include scheduling of the facility, circulation of materials and equipment, requests for consultation or instruction, and requests for production of media.

Communicating policies to students is best facilitated by a structured orientation program and frequent visits to the media center to practice applying those procedures. In schools with closed circuit television, a live or taped program concerning library media use can be very successful.

Skill 16.4 Applying knowledge of procedures for collecting and analyzing relevant quantitative and qualitative data regarding user needs to make decisions with regard to the library media program

Most school library media program evaluations have been diagnostic or qualitative. Diagnostic prescriptions alone make no allowances for specific conditions in given schools and are often interpreted too liberally; qualitative prescriptions alone are difficult to measure or sustain. Projective standards are usually broad national guidelines which serve best as long-range goals. Preferably, a program evaluation, utilizing a combination of quantitative and qualitative standards, produces results that can lead to modified objectives. Statistics to substantiate quantitative standards can be derived from:

1. Usage statistics from automated circulation systems. These indicate frequency of materials use.
2. Inventory figures. Resource turnover, loss and damage, and missing materials statistics indicate extent of use. Total materials count can substantiate materials per student criteria.
3. Individual circulation logs. Such logs indicate the frequency of patron use of library materials and the types of materials used.
4. Class scheduling log. Depending on the amount of data acquired when a visit is scheduled, several facts can be determined: proportion of staff and student body using materials and services; the frequency of use of specific resources or services; the age levels of users; specific subgroups being served; and subject matter preferences.

Evidence of meeting qualitative standards can be derived from:

1. **Lesson plans.** Careful planning will reveal the frequency of use of resources and specific classroom objectives planned cooperatively with faculty. The plan should also specify the effectiveness with which the students achieved the lesson objectives.
2. **Personnel evaluations.** Most districts have either formative evaluations, summative evaluations, or both for professional, para-professional, or non-professional staff. Student aides should receive educational credit for their services hours. Completion of specific skills and termination grades can provide both quantitative and qualitative data.
3. **Surveys.** A systematic written evaluation should be conducted annually to obtain input from students, teachers and parents on the success of program objectives.
4. **Conferences / Library Advisory Committee meetings.** Comments from faculty members and students can provide qualitative assessment of the value of the materials and services provided.
5. **Criterion-referenced or teacher made tests**. These assessments can be used to evaluate student effectiveness in acquiring information skills or content area skills.

The purposes of evaluation are to determine if all aspects of planning and implementation have been successfully accomplished. If evaluation shows unsuccessful outcomes, then the program must be modified. Successful outcomes can be used to confirm program objectives and to promote the media center programs.

Some strategies for the use of program evaluation include:
1. To produce an annual report to be included in the school's annual report to parents or other publications for circulation in the community.
2. To review and modify long-range goals and plan immediate changes in short-range goals.
3. To lobby for budgetary or personnel support.
4. To solicit assistance from faculty and administration in making curricular or instructional changes to maximize use of media center materials, equipment, and services.
5. To plan greater involvement of students in academic and personal use of media center materials and services.

Because there is currently an abundance of outstanding resource that is easily accessible through technology, evaluation can be managed by following a few simple steps.

1. Rely on the information provided in this guide's resource list. If your school or district's professional library does not contain these resources, visit the public library in the nearest large city or a university library where information sciences are taught.
2. Give your school media program a close examination before doing your research. Study any written evaluations by media personnel, school improvement committees, library advisory committees, or annual reports. Informally survey a cross-section of students and teachers to gather input about their perceptions of the materials and services that are provided.
3. Make a list of questions based on the concerns that result from your evaluation. Peruse the questions in Chapter One of *Information Power* to see if there are any pertinent areas that have not yet been addressed.
4. Do your research.
5. Produce a written evaluation of your school's library media program based on your findings. Submit this evaluation to the principal and plan with her the best way to communicate the information to students, teachers, and parents.
6. Gather input from all groups to whom your evaluation is presented.
7. Meet with the Library Media Advisory Committee or equivalent group to formulate program changes. Be sure to include students and parents or lay community members on this committee.
8. Implement the changes and plan subsequent evaluations.

TEACHER CERTIFICATION STUDY GUIDE

RESOURCES

1. American Association of School Librarians and Association for Educational Communications and Technology. *Information Power: Guidelines for School Library Media Programs.* Chicago: American Library Association and Association for Educational Communications and Technology, 1988.

   A sourcebook for presenting professional guidelines for developing school library media programs for the 1990's and into the twentieth century. It includes chapters on establishing and maintaining a school library media program; defining the role of the school library media professional and paraprofessional personnel; determining the resources, equipment and facilities necessary to meet the goals; and spelling out leadership responsibilities of district, region and state. Appendices contain policy statements of different organizations, present research results, and provide budget formulas and minimum standards for facilities spaces.

2. American Association of School Librarians and Association for Educational Communication and Technology. *Information Power: Building Partnerships for Learning.* Chicago: American Library Association and Association for Educational Communications and Technology, 1998.

   A follow-up to the publication *Information Power: Guidelines for School Library Media Programs*. It includes chapters on information literacy, collaboration, learning and teaching, information access, program administration, and connecting with the learning community. The appendices contain information on various statements and policies from various organizations.

3. American Library Association, Canadian Library Association, and The Library Association. *Anglo-American Cataloging Rules.* 2nd ed. Chicago: American Library Association, 1988.

   A revised edition which provides rules for including technology changes.

4. American Library Association, Office for Intellectual Freedom Staff. *Intellectual Freedom Manual* . 2nd ed. Chicago: American Library Association, 1983.

   Updated in 1998, this manual presents the statements of rights of various library organizations, provides the ALA Intellectual Freedom statement and its implications for library media programs, discusses laws and court cases, advises on methods to deal with censorship, and presents promotion techniques.

5. Anderson, Pauline H. *Planning School Library Media Facilities*. Hamden, CT: The Shoe String Press, Inc., 1990.

   This extensive work traces the creation of a school library media center from politicking to moving in. Much emphasis is placed on the planning process. Five specific case studies are offered to show how the process works.

6. Baker, Philipd. *The Library Media Center and the School*. Littleton, CO: Libraries Unlimited, 1984.

   A thorough discussion of the school library media program in relation to the total school mission and objectives.

7. Bannister, Barbara Farley and Janiceb. Carlile. *Elementary School Librarian's Survival Guide.* New York: The Center for Applied Research in Education, 1993.

   A great guide for either setting up a new media center or operating an existing one. It deals with the physical management of the media center; successful discipline; reading promotions; special programs; story times, book talks and library skills; building support with the school community; budgeting; selection procedures; new technologies; inventory and weeding; and avoiding burnout. Full of practical suggestions and reproducibles.

8. Brown, J. W.; R.b. Lewis; and F. F. Harcleroad. *A V Introduction: Technology, Media, and Methods.* 6th ed. New York: McGraw-Hill, 1983.

   A good reference book on the use of instructional materials and technology at all educational levels. It provides information on planning instruction, using and producing various media, operating audio-visual equipment, and designing facilities for using media. It also provides information on copyright laws.

9. Buchanan, Jan. *Flexible Access Media Programs.* Littleton, CO: Libraries Unlimited, 1991.

    A fine reference tool for understanding and developing approaches to designing flexible access programs for school library media centers. Presents an overview of current research on integrating the teaching of library skills into the curriculum, a whole language approach to teaching reading, and the importance of encouraging critical thinking. The book's greatest value is showing the building level media specialist the techniques for involving the total school community in the planning and implementation of integrated lessons and defining the roles of all the participants involved in the planning, execution and evaluation stages. Emphasis is on the cooperative planning required and on the measurable benefit to the learner.

10. Bucher, Katherine Toth. *Computers & Technology in School Library Media Centers.* Worthington, OH: Linworth Publishing, Inc., 1994.

    This 3-ring bound publication offers a thorough discussion of technology's relevance to libraries. It includes as contents (1) working with instructional technology in the 1990's, (2) computer basics, (3) library management with a computer, (4) multimedia CD-ROM, (5) videodisks in the library.

11. Carlsen, G. Robert. *Books and the Teenage Reader.* New York: Harper and Row, 1971.

    This ageless work discusses teenage interests and social/personal needs and provides reading lists in different genres, interest areas, classics, etc.

12. Donelson, K. L. anda. P. Nilsen. *Literature for Today's Young Adults.* 3rd ed. Glenview, IL: Scott, Foresman, 1989.

    A textbook dealing with print media: the history and trends of young adult literature; genres of special interest; using materials with young adults; and guidelines for evaluating these works. Presents brief statements about works of both recognized merit and potential interest to young adults and sketches of authors known in the field.

13. Downing, Mildred Harlow and David H. Downing. *Introduction to Cataloging and Classification.* 6th ed. Jefferson, NC: McFarland & Company, Inc., 1992.

    A basic primer on cataloguing techniques and classification systems.

14. Georgia Library Media Association, Inc.. 2003. Georgia Library Media Association. 1 Aug 2007 <http://glma-inc.org/index.htm>.

    Resources from Georgia's library media professional organization.

15. "Georgia Standards." Georgia Standards.Org: One Stop Shop for Educators. 2005-2006. Georgia Department of Education. 1 Aug 2007 <http://www.georgiastandards.org/>.

    Curriculum resources and standards for the state of Georgia.

16. Gillespie, J. T. (Ed.) *Best Books for Junior High Readers*. New Providence, NJ: Bowker, 1991.

    A reference guide to selecting titles for junior high (upper middle school) readers. Presents examples of literature within certain genres, discusses themes appropriate to middle grade readers based on personal, social and academic needs.

17. Gillespie, J. T. and L. Spirt. *Administering the School Library Media Center*. New York: Bowker, 1983.

    A guide to practical considerations in operating a school library media center. Chapters on acquisition, organization, and management, with chapters on new technologies. Presents example of a policies and procedures manual. Revised in 1993.

18. Hagler, Ronald. *The Bibliographic Record and Information Technology*. 2nd ed. Chicago, IL: American Library Association, 1991.

    A serious, detailed study of cataloging, bibliographic standards and controls using MARC record format.

19. Hannigan, J.A. and Glenn Estes. *Media Center Facilities Design*. Chicago, IL: American Library Association, 1978.

    Expanding on the ALA discussion of facilities design in *Information Power* these authors have presented methods and models for media facilities for all school levels, discussing factors for planning, design and construction. They even offering architectural renderings.

20. Hart, Thomas. *Behavior Management in the School Library Media Center*. Chicago, IL: American Library Association, 1985.

    A serious work on the positive educational strategies for managing student behavior in the use the resources and services of the school library media center.

21. Haycock, Ken. "Research in Teacher-Librarianship and the Institutionalization of Change." *School Library Media Quarterly* (Summer 1995): 227-233.

    This paper contends that there is ample research to prove the relationship between student achievement and the instructional role of library media specialist. Mr. Haycock offers this evidence and a 92 item annotation to point out the strong statistical support that can be used to promote programs.

22. *The School Library Program in the Curriculum*. Englewood CO: Libraries Unlimited, Inc., 1990.

    This collection of essays/opinion papers by Haycock and others deals with the media center in the context of the total school, the role of the teacher librarian, program planning and development, integrating information skills across the curriculum, secondary school applications, and issues and concerns.

23. Heinrich, R.; M. Molenda; and J.d. Russell. *Instructional Media and the New Technologies of Instruction*. 2nd ed. New York: Macmillan, 1985.

    A textbook source for planning and use of non-print media. Full of charts, diagrams and appendices on sources for free and inexpensive materials.

24. Helm, V. M. *What Educators Should Know About Copyright*. Phi Delta Kappa Educational Foundation, 1986.

    A brief, but thorough, discussion of copyright law, the court cases that have tested that law, and the implications of the rulings on schools, including library media programs.

25. Huck, C. S.; S. Hepler; and J. Hickman. *Children's Literature in the Elementary School*. 4th ed. New York: Holt, Rhinehart and Winston, 1987.

    Both a textbook in child development and the literature designed to meet children's needs, a study of genres, and a presentation of methods for teaching children's literature. Lists of book awards, authors, illustrators, periodicals and publishers.

26. Inter, Sheila S. *Circulation Policy in Academic, Public, and School Libraries*. New York: Greenwood Press, 1987.

    This book deals with circulation policies in academic, public, and school libraries. Specific circulation plans from schools around the country offer models.

27. Inter, Sheila S. and Jean Weichs. *Standard Cataloguing for School and Public Libraries*. Englewood, CO: Libraries Unlimited, 1990.

    Written for public librarians and school library media specialists, this book explains the principles and standards of cataloging. Though a thorough discussion of AACR rules, descriptions, subject headings, classification systems, etc., the book avoids discussing arcane details that are most likely not encountered by the intended audience.

28. "K-12 Library Media Services." Georgia Department of Education Projects and Programs. Georgia Department of Education. 1 Aug 2007 <http://www.glc.k12.ga.us/pandp/media/homepg.htm>.

    An overview and list of resources for Georgia's K-12 libraries.

29. Katz, W.A. *Introduction to Reference Work*. (Vol. 1) Basic Information Sources. 5th ed. New York: McGraw Hill, 1987.

    A study of traditional basic reference sources and methods for using these sources to answer reference questions. Includes an overview of the reference process and on-line reference services and their applications.

30. Kemp, J. E. *Planning and Producing Audio-visual Materials*. 4th ed. New York: Harper & Row, 1980.

    Practical guide to media production techniques and methods of instruction. Summarizes research on the effectiveness of instructional materials and explains the method of developing an instructional program.

31. Kinney, Lisa F. *Lobby for Your Library-Know What Works*. Chicago, IL: American Library Association, 1992.

    Chapter 8 deals specifically with lobbying for schools, presenting typical funding sources and offering strategies to be used by key participants in lobbying agencies from local to state.

32. Klasing, Jane P. *Designing and Renovating School Library Media Centers*. Chicago, IL: American Library Association, 1991.

    A quick reference for use by school personnel in planning and implementing an efficient facilities design. Sample floor plans and appendices full of bid forms, architectural symbols and furniture details simplify the process.

33. Lance, Keith Curry. *The Impact of School Library Media Centers on Academic Achievement*. Castle Rock, CO: Willow Research and Publishing, 1993.

    Predominantly a research-based discussion of factors of library media programs that have directly influenced the improvement in student grades, standardized scores and self-directed learning.

34. Laughlin, Mildred Knight and Kathy Howard Latrobe. (Eds.) *Public Relations for School Library Media Centers.* Englewood, CO: Libraries Unlimited, 1990.

    Seventeen articles about different facets of promoting the school library media program, including definitions of public relations, the library media specialist's attitude and interpersonal skills, stress and public relations, and specific groups to motivate.

35. Loertscher, D.V. *Taxonomies of the School Library Media Program*. Englewood, CO: Libraries Unlimited, 1988.

    One of the most outstanding works on elements of the school library media center program. Outlines the roles of media professionals, students, teachers and administrators in integrating the library media program into the school curriculum. Models for personnel and program evaluation are included in appendices.

36. Pillon, N.B. *Reaching Young People Through Media*. Littleton, CO: Libraries Unlimited, 1983.

    Fifteen articles dealing with such topics as reading interests, materials selection, genres, censorship, youth advocacy, and technology.

37. Prostano, Emanuel T. and Joyce S. Prostano. *The School Library Media Center*. 3rd ed. Littleton, CO: Libraries Unlimited, 1982.

    Revised in 1987, this book deals with the library media center program development, administration and evaluation. There are also chapters on curriculum integration, media personnel, facilities and furniture, media and equipment, and the budget.

38. Reichman, Henry. *Censorship and Selection-Issues and Answers for Schools*. Chicago, IL: American Library Association, 1993.

    This book addresses the specific problems of intellectual freedom encountered in schools. It discusses issues that are in dispute, selection policies and the law. It also offers possible solutions to complaints.

39. Riggs, D.E. *Strategic Planning for Library Managers*. Phoenix, AZ: Oryx Press, 1984.

    A thorough guide for planning for all types of libraries, especially useful in discussing leadership, organization and evaluation techniques. Especially effective in defining mission statement and distinguishing between goals and objectives.

40. *School Library Media Annual*. Shirley Aaron and Pat Scales (Eds.) [1983-1987 eds.] and Jane Bandy Smith (Ed.) [1988-1990 eds.] Littleton, CO: Libraries Unlimited.

    Each volume contains articles on national and state legislation, professional organizations, government affairs and publications of note. Individual volumes highlight special issues.

    Volume 1: adolescent development, intellectual freedom, certification, instructional radio and television, software evaluations, networking.

    Volume 2: lobbying, continuing education, declining enrollment, impact of library media programs on student achievement, telecommunications.

    Volume 3: censorship; intellectual freedom committees, copyright concerns, interactive video, microcomputers in schools, ethical considerations.

    Volume 4: professionalizing the media profession; planning effective programs; information skills; facilities design; intellectual freedom, censorship, and copyright; managing on-line services.

Volume 5: copyright for new technologies; selection policies and procedures; continuing education; leadership skills; advisory committees; promoting information and inquiry skills.

Volume 6: whole language impact on media, censorship, research on library media centers, updates on automation.

Volume 7: measuring services, developing standards, personnel, flexible scheduling, accreditation, state guidelines, implementing *Information Power*, partnership of NCATE and ALA/AASL.

Volume 8: instructional consulting role, principal's role in creating vision for school library media programs, learning styles, designing effective instruction, contributions of technology, information literacy.

41. Smith, Jane Bandy. *Achieving A Curriculum-Based Library Media Center Program-The Middle School Model for Change*. Chicago, IL: American Library Association, 1995.

    This book presents information and practical models for integrating information skills into the school curriculum. This is a sequel to Smith's *Library Media Center Programs for Middle Schools.*

42. *Library Media Center Programs for Middle School: A Curriculum-Based Approach*. Chicago, IL: American Library Association, 1989.

    This book presents information on planning and evaluating middle school media programs. It offers procedures in library program development as well as ways of correlating library skills with classroom instruction.

43. Stein, Barbara L. and Risa W. Brown. *Running A School Library Media Center-A How-to-do-it Manual for Librarians*. New York: Neal-Schuman Publishers Inc., 1992.

    A practical handbook includes chapters on getting started, administration, ordering and processing materials, cataloging, circulation, maintaining the collection, hiring and working with staff, designing and using the facility, and programming the media center.

44. Sutherland, Zena and M. H. Arbuthnot. *Children and Books*. 7th ed. Glenview, IL: Scott Foresman, 1986.

Chapter One of Part One, "Children and Books Today," discusses the history and direction of children's literature, influences on children's literature, child psychology theories and their application to cognitive development. Chapter Two, "Guiding Children's Book Selection," discusses evaluation standards and examines the elements and range of children's literature. Subsequent chapters provide titles and summaries of recommended literature for various age groups.

45. Talav, Rosemary. *Common Sense Copyright*. New York: McFarland, 1986.

A practical guide to applying copyright laws in school environments, one chapter specifically addressing media centers.

46. Turner, P. M. *Helping Teachers Teach: A School Library Media Specialist's Role*. Littleton, CO: Libraries Unlimited, 1985.

An exploration of the school library media specialist's role as a curriculum consultant, with specific suggestions for methods to help teachers design and evaluate classroom lessons using media resources. Also provides information on professional collection development, instructional materials selection and evaluation, and in-house workshop design. Revised in 1988 and 1993.

47. Van Orden, Phyllis J. *The Collection Program in Schools*. Englewood, CO: Libraries Unlimited, 1988.

A textbook for media professionals on collection development. Divided into three parts: *The Setting* issues procedures and policies; *Selection of Materials* addresses selection criteria; and *Administrative Concerns* covers acquisition, maintenance, evaluation and meeting special needs.

48. Walker, H.T. and P. K. Montgomery. *Teaching Library Media Skills. An Instructional Program for Elementary and Middle School Students*. Littleton, CO: Libraries Unlimited, 1983.

Another good source for using both print and non-print sources to teach library skills. It offers subject related activities for required and elective subjects as well as discussing the aspects of instruction.

49. Wehmeyer, L.B. *The School Librarian as Educator.* 2nd ed. Littleton, CO: Libraries Unlimited, 1984.

    A text which examines the school library media specialist's role as instructor, offering practical suggestions for library skills instruction and including appendices with games and activities appropriate to both elementary and secondary media centers.

50. Winn, Patricia. *Integration of the Secondary School Library Media Center into the Curriculum.* Englewood, CO: Libraries Unlimited, 1991.

    This title specifically addresses the role of the media specialist in integrating the media program into the curriculum and some methods to use.

51. Woolls, E. Blanche and David V. Loertscher (Eds.) *The Microcomputer Facility and the School Library Media Specialist.* Chicago, IL: American Library Association, 1986.

This book is a series of essays in four areas: planning the facility, operating the facility, services of the facility, and working with the facility. From district level networks to microcomputers used for circulation, the microcomputer is here presented as a tool to ease the burden of library media management.

52. Wright, Keith. *The Challenge of Technology-Action Strategies for the school Library Media Specialist.* Chicago. IL: American Library Association, 1993.

    Mr. Wright wrote this book because of a concern that technology be used appropriately in education. He addresses the challenges that new technologies have created for the media professional, discusses techniques that schools or districts have used to deal with these challenges, and suggests ways that school library media specialists can prioritize their growing responsibilities.

SAMPLE TEST

DIRECTIONS: Read each item and select the best response.

1. A school library media specialist is searching for ways to make the school library more effective. Which of the following would not be a successful strategy?
   (Skill 1.1) Rigorous

   A. The school library media specialist develops activities that help to develop creativity and support critical thinking skills.

   B. The school library media specialist works in isolation to plan effective programs that support curriculum guidelines.

   C. The school library media specialist develops activities to expand students' interests and promote lifelong learning.

   D. The school library media specialist provides physical access to resources.

2. A statement defining the core principles of a school library media program is called the:
   (Skill 1.2) Average rigor

   A. mission

   B. policy

   C. procedure

   D. objective

3. Which version of *Information Power* was published in 1998?
   (Skill 1.2) Easy

   A. *Information Power: The Role of the School Library Media Program*

   B. *Information Power: A Review of Research*

   C. *Information Power: Guidelines for School Library Media Programs*

   D. *Information Power: Building Partnerships for Learning*

4. The school library media center should be an inviting space that encourages learning. To accomplish this, the school library media specialist should do all of the following except:
(Skill 1.3) Average rigor

   A. collaborate with school staff and students.

   B. create a schedule where each class comes to the media center each week for instruction.

   C. arrange materials so that they are easy to locate.

   D. promote the program as a wonderful place for learning.

5. All of the following organizations serve school libraries except:
(Skill 1.4) Average rigor

   A. AASL

   B. AECT

   C. ALCT

   D. ALA

6. According to the AASL-AECT national guidelines, which of the following is NOT one of the three overlapping roles of the school library media specialist?
(Skill 1.4) Average rigor

   A. information specialist.

   B. equipment technician.

   C. teacher.

   D. instructional consultant.

7. According to AASL/AECT guidelines, in his or her role as *instructional consultant,* the school library media specialist uses his or her expertise to
(Skill 1.4) Rigorous

   A. assist teachers in acquiring information skills which they can incorporate into classroom instruction.

   B. provide access to resource sharing systems.

   C. plan lessons in media production.

   D. provide staff development activities in equipment use.

8. QCC is the acronym for:
   (Skill 1.5) Easy

   A. Quality Curriculum Content

   B. Quality Classroom Curriculum

   C. Quality Core Curriculum

   D. Quality Classroom Content

9. For students to take responsibility for their own learning the media specialist much teach them all of the following but:
   (Skill 1.6) Easy

   A. locate resources.

   B. evaluate resources.

   C. purchase resources

   D. use resources.

10. When evaluating resources for effectiveness it is important to consider all of the following except:
    (Skill 2.1) Average rigor

    A. style of the web page.

    B. the intended audience.

    C. whether or not the site is from a scholarly source.

    D. the scope of the information

11. A periodical index search which allows the user to pair Keywords with <u>and</u>, <u>but</u>, or <u>or</u> is called
    (Skill 2.1) Average rigor

    A. Boolean.

    B. dialoguing.

    C. wildcarding.

    D. truncation.

12. When a new media specialist comes to a library, it is important for them to become familiar with the existing resource collection. One of the best ways to do this is to:
    (Skill 2.2) Rigorous

    A. consult the district director regarding collection policies.

    B. browse the shelves to evaluate what is available.

    C. examine collections of other comparable schools.

    D. study the school's curriculum to understand the needs of users.

13. Which of the following is the least effective way of communicating school library media policies, procedures and rules to media center patrons?
(Skill 2.5) Average rigor

    A. announcements made in faculty and parent support group meetings.

    B. a published faculty procedures manual.

    C. written guidelines in the student handbook or special media handbill.

    D. a videotape orientation viewed over the school's closed circuit television system.

14. A library procedures manual should contain which of the following?
(Skill 2.3) Average rigor

    A. mission

    B. specific media policies

    C. specific media procedures

    D. all of the above

15. All but which of the following criteria are used when determining fair use of copyrighted material for classroom use?
(Skill 2.4) Average rigor

    A. Brevity Test.

    B. Spontaneity Test.

    C. Time Test.

    D. Cumulative Effect Test.

16. Section 108 of the Copyright Act permits the copying of an entire book if three conditions are met. Which of the following is NOT one of those conditions?
(Skill 2.4) Rigorous

    A. The library intends to allow inter-library loan of the book.

    B. The library is an archival library.

    C. The copyright notice appears on all the copies.

    D. The library is a public library.

17. Under the copyright brevity test, an educator may reproduce without written permission
    (Skill 2.4) Rigorous

    A. 10% of any prose or poetry work.

    B. 500 words from a 5000 word article.

    C. 240 words of a 2400 word story.

    D. no work over 2500 words.

18. "Fair Use" policy in videotaping off-air from commercial television requires the instructor to:
    (Skill 2.4) Rigorous

    A. show in 5 days, erase by the 20th day.

    B. show in 10 days, erase by the 30th day.

    C. show in 10 days, erase by the 45th day.

    D. no restrictions.

19. Licensing has become a popular means of copyright protection in the area of
    (Skill 2.4) Average rigor

    A. duplicating books for interlibrary loan.

    B. use of software application on multiple machines.

    C. music copying.

    D. making transparency copies of books or workbooks that are too expensive to purchase.

20. Which of the following is a file extension for a video file?
    (Skill 2.5) Average rigor

    A. .mp3

    B. .wav

    C. .avi

    D. .jpeg

21. Which writer composes young adult literature in the fantasy genre?
    (Skill 3.1) Rigorous

    A. Stephen King.

    B. Piers Anthony.

    C. Virginia Hamilton.

    D. Phyllis Whitney.

MEDIA SPECIALIST

22. Which fiction genre do authors Isaac Asimov, Louise Lawrence and Andre Norton represent?
    (Skill 3.1) Rigorous

    A. adventure.

    B. romance.

    C. science fiction.

    D. fantasy.

23. All of the following are authors of young adult fiction EXCEPT
    (Skill 3.1) Rigorous

    A. Paul Zindel.

    B. Norma Fox Mazer.

    C. S.E. Hinton.

    D. Maurice Sendak

24. The award given for the best children's literature (text) is:
    (Skill 3.1) Easy

    A. the Caldecott.

    B. the Newbery.

    C. the Pulitzer.

    D. the Booklist.

25. Which book was selected as the Georgia Book Award Winner for the picture book category in 2004-05?
    (Skill 3.1) Rigorous

    A. *Stanley's Party* by Linda Bailey and Bill Slavin

    B. *Bark, George* by Jules Feiffer

    C. *No, David* by David Shannon

    D. *Loser* by Jerry Spinelli

26. To foster the collaborative process the media specialist must possess all of the following skills except:
    (Skill 3.2) Easy

    A. leadership

    B. flexibility

    C. perversity

    D. persistence

TEACHER CERTIFICATION STUDY GUIDE

27. The role of the Media Committee or Media Advisory Committee is to assist with all of the following except:
    (Skill 3.2) Average rigor

    A. determine program direction

    B. evaluate the media specialist

    C. direct budget decisions

    D. collaborate with the media specialist

28. When selecting books for students in grades k-2, it is best to choose books with which of the following characteristics?
    (Skill 3.3) Easy

    A. strong picture support

    B. familiar language patterns

    C. utilize cuing systems

    D. all of the above

29. *The Horn Book* is
    (Skill 3.4) Average rigor

    A. a book about trumpets

    B. a children's picture book

    C. a professional journal

    D. a source for resource reviews

30. Which of these publications does not contain reviews for various types of publications:
    (Skill 3.4) Average rigor

    A. School Library Journal

    B. Booklist

    C. Media Center Review

    D. The Horn Book

31. Literature appreciation activities can include which of the following:
    (Skill 3.5) Easy

    A. author studies

    B. genre studies

    C. book talks

    D. all of the above

32. Factors that influence the atmosphere of a library media center contain all of the following except:
    (Skill 4.1) Average rigor

    A. aesthetic appearance

    B. acoustical ceiling and floor coverings.

    C. size of the media center

    D. proximity to classrooms

MEDIA SPECIALIST

33. *Information Power: Building Partnerships for Learning* recommends flexible scheduling for
    (Skill 4.2) Easy

    A. elementary school library media centers.

    B. middle school library media centers.

    C. secondary school library media centers.

    D. all school library media centers.

34. When creating a schedule for a school library media center the type of schedule that maximizes access to resources is a:
    (Skill 4.2) Easy

    A. fixed schedule

    B. open schedule

    C. partial fixed schedule

    D. flexible schedule

35. Contemporary library media design models should consider which of the following?
    (Skill 4.3) Rigorous

    A. flexibility of space to allow for reading, viewing, and listening.

    B. space for large group activities such as district meetings, standardized testing, and lectures.

    C. traffic flow patterns for entrance and exit from the media center as well as easy movement within the center.

    D. adequate and easy to rearrange storage areas for the variety of media formats and packaging style of modern materials.

36. The most important consideration in the design of a new school library media center is
    (Skill 4.3) Rigorous

    A. the goals of the library media center program.

    B. the location of the facility on the school campus.

    C. state standards for facilities use.

    D. the demands of current technologies.

37. The ADA Accessibility Guidelines for Buildings and Facilities recommends that a media center allows *how much aisle space?*
    (Skill 4.3) Rigorous

    A. 41 inches

    B. 42 inches

    C. 43 inches

    D. 44 inches

38. Key design elements to consider when renovating or building a new facility include:
    (Skill 4.4) Average rigor

    A. Traffic flow

    B. Access for physically impaired users

    C. Security needs

    D. all of the above

39. A cooperative relationship between a media specialist and a teacher is known as:
    (Skill 4.5) Average rigor

    A. collection development

    B. collaboration

    C. telecommunications

    D. flexible scheduling

40. Which of the following is an example of quantitative data that would be used to evaluate a school library media program?
    (Skill 4.6) Average rigor

    A. Personnel evaluations

    B. Usage statistics

    C. Surveys

    D. Interviews

41. An accredited elementary school has maintained an acceptable number of items in its print collection for ten years. In the evaluation review, this fact is evidence of both
    (Skill 4.6) Rigorous

    A. diagnostic and projective standards.

    B. diagnostic and quantitative standards.

    C. projective and quantitative standards.

    D. projective and qualitative standards.

42. The principal is completing the annual report. He needs to include substantive data on use of the media center. In addition to the number of book circulations, he or she would like to know the proportionate use of the media center's facilities and services by the various grade levels or content areas. This information can most quickly be obtained from:
(Skill 4.6) Rigorous

   A. the class scheduling log.

   B. student surveys.

   C. lesson plans.

   D. inventory figures.

43. The ACLU's mission is to preserve First Amendment rights for all Americans. ACLU is the acronym for which organization:
(Skill 4.7) Easy

   A. American Curricular Libraries Union

   B. American Civil Libraries Union

   C. American Civil Liberties Union

   D. American Curricular Liberties Union

44. In the landmark U.S. Supreme Court ruling in favor of Pico, the court's opinion established that
(Skill 4.7) Rigorous

   A. library books, being optional, not required reading, could not be arbitrarily removed by school boards.

   B. school boards have the same jurisdiction over library books as they have over textbooks.

   C. the intent to remove pervasively vulgar material is the same as the intent to deny free access to ideas.

   D. First Amendment challenges in regards to library books are the responsibility of appeals courts.

45. The two main categories of print resources found in most libraries are:
(Skill 5.1, 14.1) Average rigor

   A. reference and circulating materials

   B. picture books and chapter books

   C. reference books and picture books

   D. encyclopedias and chapter books

46. What is one advantage of keeping print resources in a media collection?
    (Skill 5.2) Rigorous

    A. Information is easier to find in print resources.

    B. Young children need to learn how to use a book.

    C. Print materials last a long time.

    D. Print materials are interactive

47. A search that uses specific terms to locate information is called a:
    (Skill 5.3) Average rigor

    A. reference search

    B. keyword search

    C. ready reference search

    D. operator search

48. Which of the following searches would most likely return the most results?
    (Skill 5.4) Average rigor

    A. lions AND tigers

    B. lions NOT tigers

    C. lions OR tigers

    D. lions AND NOT tigers

49. A request from a social studies class for the creation of a list of historical fiction titles for a book report assignment is a _____ request.
    (Skill 5.5) Rigorous

    A. ready reference

    B. research

    C. specific needs

    D. complex search

50. All of the following are periodical directories except:
    (Skill 5.5) Average rigor

    A. *Ulrich's*

    B. *TNYT*

    C. *SIRS*

    D. *PAIS*

51. When evaluating resources for effectiveness it is important to consider all of the following except:
    (Skill 6.1) Rigorous

    A. style of the web page.

    B. the intended audience.

    C. whether or not the site is from a scholarly source.

    D. the scope of the information

52. In most learning hierarchies, which of the following is the lowest order critical thinking skill?
    (Skill 6.2) Average rigor

    A. appreciation.

    B. inference.

    C. recall.

    D. comprehension

53. After reading *The Pearl,* a tenth grader asks, "Why can't we start sentences with *and* like John Steinbeck?" This student is showing the ability to
    (Skill 6.2) Rigorous

    A. appreciate.

    B. comprehend.

    C. infer.

    D. evaluate.

54. In most learning hierarchies, which of the following is the highest order critical thinking skill?
    (Skill 6.2) Average rigor

    A. appreciation.

    B. inference.

    C. recall.

    D. comprehension.

55. In the production of a teacher/student made audio-visual material, which of the following is NOT a factor in the planning phase?
    (Skill 6.3) Rigorous

    A. stating the objectives.

    B. analyzing the audience.

    C. determining the purpose.

    D. selecting the format.

56. Which of the following formats is best for large group presentations?
    (Skill 6.4) Easy

    A. manipulatives

    B. multimedia

    C. audio recordings

    D. photographs

57. All of the following formats are best for small group learning except:
    (Skill 6.4) Average rigor

    A. manipulatives

    B. computer projection

    C. photographs

    D. computer software

58. Which of the following is a popular format for citing resources?
    (Skill 6.5) Rigorous

    A. CMA

    B. APA

    C. DMA

    D. MPA

59. MLA style is a popular format for citing resources in a bibliography. MLA is the acronym for:
    (Skill 6.5) Rigorous

    A. Media Library Association

    B. Modern Library Association

    C. Modern Literary Association

    D. Modern Language Association

60. A scoring guide that is generally subjective and contains specific criteria in which projects should be judged is known as a:
    (Skill 6.6) Easy

    A. rubric

    B. outline

    C. criteria

    D. evaluation

61. As instructors, school library media specialists must be able to construct statements of objectives for instructional purposes. Which of the following is a properly stated objective?
    (Skill 7.1) Rigorous

    A. To describe the process necessary to locate books on Third World countries in the reference area.

    B. To demonstrate the use of the library's automated catalog to aid a newcomer in determining whether a particular title is available.

    C. To understand how the Dewey Decimal System works.

    D. To identify ten authors who have contributed to economic, social, or cultural changes in the 20th century.

62. When working with patrons to determine their specific information needs it may be necessary to ask the patron a series of questions that uncover needs, often called a:
    (Skill 7.2) Rigorous

    A. ready reference request

    B. special needs request

    C. reference interview

    D. evaluation interview

63. Which of the following would be a good question to ask during a reference interview?
    (Skill 7.2) Rigorous

    A. Do you have a topic?

    B. What is your topic?

    C. Have you located any resources regarding your topic?

    D. Do you know where to go to find the information?

64. Howard Gardner is responsible for the creation of
    (Skill 7.3) Easy

    A. Multiple Intelligences

    B. Taxonomies of Learning

    C. Big 6 Model

    D. @ Your Library

65. Which of the following would be an example of an activity that would use the Bloom's taxonomy level of Recall or Knowledge?
    (Skill 7.3) Average rigor

    A. Producing a presentation.

    B. Retelling a story.

    C. Rewriting the ending of a story.

    D. React to the author's language or style.

66. Authentic learning activities have students explore curricular objectives in the context of real world problems and projects. Which of the following is not an example of this type of activity?
    (Skill 7.4) Rigorous

    A. Students create a brochure to make people aware of the needs of the community's food bank.

    B. Students help the school create advertisements for an upcoming school event.

    C. Students research a character found in a book they've read.

    D. Students monitor and report on the water quality of a local pond or lake.

67. Skills that provide students with the ability to solve problems are known as
    (Skill 7.5) Average rigor

    A. critical thinking skills

    B. multiple intelligences

    C. Loertscher's Taxonomies

    D. authentic learning

68. When creating instructional materials which of the following is not a part of the planning phase?
    (Skill 7.6) Rigorous

    A. determining the goal or objectives to be covered

    B. creating the media

    C. analyzing the audience

    D. determining the purpose

69. Collaboration between the media specialist and classroom teacher is the key to an effective library media program. Which of the following scenarios best describes a media specialist willing to foster a collaborative partnership with a teacher?
    (Skill 8.1) Rigorous

    A. The media specialist meets only when approached by a classroom teacher who is asking for help.

    B. The media specialist can only meet on Tuesdays and Thursdays from 1-2 due to the fixed schedule that has been set up for the media center.

    C. The media specialist touches base with teachers on a regular basis and attends grade level planning sessions.

    D. The media specialist only meets with teachers on each grade level who are interested in working collaboratively.

70. Media specialists can assist teachers with the teaching of reading by assessing students' reading habits. Tools that can be used to accomplish this task include:
(Skill 8.2) Easy

   A. interviews

   B. surveys

   C. packaged assessment programs

   D. all of the above

71. As much as possible, information skills should be taught as
(Skill 8.3) Easy

   A. lessons independent of content studies.

   B. lessons to supplement content studies.

   C. lessons integrated into content studies.

   D. lessons enriched by content studies.

72. The creators of the Big 6 Model are:
(Skill 8.3) Average rigor

   A. Eisenberg and Berkowitz.

   B. Marzano and Bloom.

   C. Bloom and Gardner.

   D. Lance and Eisenberg.

73. The capability to understand when information is needed and to identify, evaluate, and use the information effectively is known as:
(Skill 8.3) Rigorous

   A. Collaborative partnership

   B. Information literacy

   C. Taxonomies of literacy

   D. Bloom's Taxonomies

74. Steps in the Big 6 Model include all of the following except:
(Skill 8.3) Rigorous

   A. information seeking strategies

   B. location and access

   C. creation of information

   D. task definition

75. Another popular information literacy model is:
(Skill 8.3) Rigorous

   A. Bloom's Taxonomies

   B. Star Reader

   C. Pathways to Knowledge

   D. Follett Taxonomies

76. Students with disabilities would benefit from specialized software that can read online text, PDF documents and scanned pages. One popular software title is called:
(Skill 8.4) Rigorous

   A. Kurzweil Reader

   B. Accelerated Reader

   C. Star Reader

   D. Kertfeld Reader

77. The media specialist needs to expand the collection to include a wider variety of resources for visually impaired students. Which of the following would be least beneficial?
(Skill 8.4) Average rigor

   A. Books with larger print.

   B. Books in Braille format.

   C. Books in audio format.

   D. Books in video format.

78. Web page editing software that allows the user to preview web pages as they are being created is called:
(Skill 8.5) Average rigor

   A. WYSWYG

   B. WYSIYG

   C. WISWYG

   D. WYSIWYG

79. Software designed to organize, manage and retrieve resources quickly and easily is called:
(Skill 8.5) Average rigor

   A. database

   B. spreadsheet

   C. word processing

   D. teleconference

80. Software that allows users to communicate over the Internet using audio and/or video is called:
(Skill 8.5) Rigorous

   A. database

   B. spreadsheet

   C. web editor

   D. teleconferencing

81. One key component of the National Board for Professional Teaching Standards for Library Media is self reflection. Which of the following is the best definition of self reflection? *(Skill 8.6) Rigorous*

   A. The process that guides one through examination of previous activities and helps one to propose improvements for the future.

   B. The process that guides one through examination of current activities and helps one to propose improvements for past activities.

   C. The process that guides one through examination of previous activities and helps one propose improvements for past activities.

   D. The process that guides one through examination of future activities and helps one propose improvements for future activities.

82. A general statement or outcome that is broken down into specific skills is known as a: *(Skill 9.1) Average rigor*

   A. policy

   B. procedure

   C. goal

   D. objective

83. When working to improve student instruction, the media specialist should work collaboratively with which groups? *(Skill 9.2) Easy*

   A. grade level

   B. school curriculum committee

   C. district curriculum committee

   D. all of the above

84. The media specialist is interested in beginning collaborative planning sessions with the teachers within the school, but not all of the teachers are interested. The media specialist should:
(Skill 9.3) Average rigor

    A. wait until all of the teachers are interested

    B. have the principal make all teacher collaboratively plan with the media specialist

    C. work with the teachers who are most willing to engage in the process

    D. abandon the idea

85. The American Library Association defines four levels of collaboration. The four levels are coordination, cooperation, integrated instruction and:
(Skill 9.4) Rigorous

    A. cooperative grouping

    B. independent instruction

    C. integrated curriculum

    D. instructional partnership

86. Collaborative partnerships with staff can take on many forms. All of the following are examples of partnerships except:
(Skill 9.5) Rigorous

    A. serving on curriculum development committees

    B. viewing the school's curriculum and creating lessons

    C. assisting teachers in planning, designing, and teaching lessons

    D. assisting teachers and students with the use of new technologies

87. The practice of examining the quantity and quality of the school library media resource collection which provides a "snapshot" of the collection is called:
(Skill 9.6) Easy

    A. collection development

    B. collection maintenance

    C. collection mapping

    D. weeding

88. Current trends in school library media include all of the following except:
(Skill 10.1) Easy

    A. use of Internet

    B. face to face instruction

    C. developing partnerships

    D. use of electronic books

89. Two information literacy models are:
(Skill 10.2) Rigorous

    A. Big 6 and Bloom's

    B. Bloom's and Loertscher

    C. Loertscher and ISearch

    D. Big 6 and ISearch

90. Staff development is most effective when it includes:
(Skill 10.3) Average rigor

    A. continuing support

    B. hand-outs

    C. video tutorials

    D. stated objectives

91. Research that examines current teaching strategies and searches for ways to improve upon them is known as:
(Skill 10.4) Rigorous

    A. quantitative research

    B. qualitative research

    C. action research

    D. procedural research

92. A good leader should:
(Skill 11.1) Easy

    A. delegate responsibility

    B. show respect for colleagues

    C. engage in continuing education

    D. all of the above

93. When implementing new technologies it is important for the media specialist to model its use. It is also important for the media specialist to:
    (Skill 11.2) Average rigor

    A. Send updated hand-outs to staff.

    B. Provide web resources to assist with utilization of the tool.

    C. Provide brief refresher modules.

    D. All of the above.

94. Which of the following is an example of quantitative data that would be used to evaluate a school library media program?
    (Skill 11.4) Average rigor

    A. Personnel evaluations

    B. Usage statistics

    C. Surveys

    D. Interviews

95. Evaluation criteria that presents guidelines for conditions as they ought to be ideally is known as:
    (Skill 11.4) Rigorous

    A. diagnostic standards.

    B. quantitative standards.

    C. projective standards.

    D. qualitative standards.

96. Lesson plans, Personnel evaluations, Surveys, Conferences, and Criterion-referenced or teacher made tests are forms of which standard:
    (Skill 11.4) Average rigor

    A. diagnostic standards.

    B. quantitative standards.

    C. projective standards.

    D. qualitative standards.

97. Which of the following is not a benefit of forming partnerships within the community?
    (Skill 11.5) Average rigor

    A. increased support for media program

    B. decline in media resources

    C. provide wide array of resources

    D. increase parental involvement

98. Partners for a school library media program may include:
    (Skills 11.5) Easy

    A. universities

    B. local businesses

    C. community organizations

    D. all of the above

99. A network allows which of the following to occur?
    (Skill 12.1) Average rigor

    A. sharing files.

    B. sharing printers.

    C. sharing software.

    D. all of the above

100. The online virtual library for Georgia that was developed by the Board of Regents of the University System of Georgia is called:
    (Skill 12.1) Easy

    A. GALILEO

    B. GSLMA

    C. GAIT

    D. GSPRA

101. School libraries may wish to form partnerships with outside organizations for all of the following reasons except: (Skill 12.2) Rigorous

    A. narrow student learning experience.

    B. diminish financial support for library or school projects.

    C. eliminate the need for the school library media specialist to be involved in the community

    D. none of the above

102. A catalog that contains materials from several library collections is known as a:
    (Skill 12.3) Average rigor

    A. Shared Catalog.

    B. Cooperative Catalog.

    C. Union Catalog.

    D. Universal Catalog.

103. Resources can be shared within a small geographic location such as a school by the use of a:
(Skill 12.4) Average rigor

    A. SWN.

    B. MAN.

    C. LAN.

    D. WAN.

104. Which professional journal is published by the American Association of School Librarians.
(Skill 12.5) Rigorous

    A. School Library Media Research

    B. Library Trends

    C. Library Power

    D. Voices of Youth Advocate

105. IRA is the acronym for the:
(Skill 12.5) Easy

    A. Interactive Reading Administration.

    B. International Reading Administration.

    C. International Reading Association.

    D. Interactive Reading Association.

106. Which of the following is NOT one of three general criteria for selection of all materials?
(Skill 13.1) Average rigor

    A. authenticity.

    B. appeal.

    C. appropriateness.

    D. allocation.

107. Collection development policies are developed to accomplish all of the following except
(Skill 13.1) Rigorous

    A. guarantee users freedom to access information.

    B. recognize the needs and interests of users.

    C. coordinate selection criteria and budget concerns.

    D. recognize rights of individuals or groups to challenge these policies.

108. The process of discarding worn or outdated books and materials is known as:
(Skill 13.2) Easy

    A. weeding.

    B. inventory.

    C. collection mapping.

    D. eliminating.

109. **An acronym that is often used to remind media specialists of the steps to weeding a collection is:**
(Skill 13.2) Average rigor

    A. WEAR.

    B. MUSTIE.

    C. ABCD.

    D. RIPPED.

110. **MARC is the acronym for:**
(Skill 13.3) Easy

    A. Mobile Accessible Recorded Content

    B. Machine Accessible Readable Content

    C. Machine Readable Content

    D. Mobile Accessible Readable Content

111. **AACR2 is the acronym for:**
(Skill 13.3) Average rigor

    A. Anglo-American Cataloging Rules Second Edition

    B. American Association of Cataloging Rules Second Edition

    C. American Association of Content Rules Second Edition

    D. Anglo-American Content Rules Second Edition

112. **All of the following are components of a circulation policy except:**
(Skill 13.4) Rigorous

    A. loan period

    B. process for handling overdues

    C. limitations

    D. location to post borrower's name

113. **When automating a library catalog it is important to consider which of the following prior to set up?**
(Skill 13.5) Average rigor

    A. technical requirements

    B. loan period

    C. patron limitations

    D. color of spine labels

114. **When determining a specific piece of equipment to purchase, the school library media specialist should first consult**
(Skill 14.2) Rigorous

    A. local vendors for a demonstration.

    B. reviews in technology periodicals.

    C. manufacturers' catalogs for specifications.

    D. the state bid list for price.

115. When new technologies arrive at the school it is most important to:
    (Skill 14.3) Average rigor

    A. inventory the item

    B. catalog the item

    C. train teachers to use the item

    D. do nothing.

116. The Position Statement on Flexible Scheduling was developed by :
    (Skill 14.4) Rigorous

    A. AASL

    B. ALA

    C. AECT

    D. SLMA

117. Which of the following should participate in the development of local policies and procedures:
    (Skill 15.1) Average rigor

    A. teacher

    B. student

    C. parents

    D. all of the above

118. According to research on promotion techniques and support for library media programs, their staunchest ally must be the
    (Skill 15.2) Rigorous

    A. teaching faculty.

    B. student body.

    C. district media supervisor.

    D. school principal.

119. In a school with one full-time library media assistant (clerk), which of the following are responsibilities of the assistant?
    (Skill 15.3) Rigorous

    A. selecting and ordering titles for the print collection.

    B. performing circulation tasks and processing new materials.

    C. in servicing teachers on the integration of media materials into the school curriculum.

    D. planning and implementing programs to involve parents and community.

120. In formulating an estimated collection budget consider all of the following except
(Skill 15.4) Rigorous

    A. attrition by loss, damage, or age.

    B. the maximum cost of item replacement.

    C. the number of students served.

    D. the need for expansion to meet minimum guidelines.

121. The most appropriate means of obtaining extra funds for library media programs is
(Skill 15.5) Average rigor

    A. having candy sales.

    B. conducting book fairs.

    C. charging fines.

    D. soliciting donations.

122. Long range plans should span how many years?
(Skill 16.1) Easy

    A. 2 – 4

    B. 3 – 5

    C. 5 – 10

    D. 10 – 15

123. The Georgia agencies that have worked together to align services and standards pertaining to media programs are:
(Skill 16.2) Rigorous

    A. Georgia Library Association and the Georgia Department of Education

    B. Georgia Library Association and Georgia Association for Instructional Technology

    C. Georgia Department of Education and Georgia Association of Instructional Technology

    D. Georgia Media Specialists Association and the Georgia Department of Education

124. Policies that determine procedures for copyright laws and reproduction of materials are generally determined at which level:
(Skill 16.3) Average rigor

    A. grade level

    B. school level

    C. community level

    D. district level

125. The most efficient method of assessing which students are users or non-users of the library media center is reviewing (Skill 16.4 (Average Rigor)

    A. patron circulation records

    B. needs assessment surveys of students.

    C. monthly circulation statistics.

    D. the accession book for the current year.

Answer Key:

1. B	33. D	65. B	97. B
2. A	34. D	66. C	98. D
3. D	35. B	67. A	99. D
4. B	36. A	68. B	100. A
5. C	37. B	69. B	101. D
6. B	38. D	70. D	102. C
7. D	39. B	71. C	103. C
8. C	40. B	72. A	104. A
9. C	41. B	73. B	105. C
10. A	42. A	74. C	106. D
11. A	43. C	75. C	107. C
12. B	44. A	76. A	108. A
13. A	45. A	77. D	109. B
14. D	46. B	78. D	110. C
15. C	47. B	79. A	111. A
16. A	48. C	80. D	112. D
17. B	49. C	81. A	113. A
18. C	50. B	82. C	114. C
19. B	51. A	83. D	115. C
20. C	52. C	84. C	116. A
21. B	53. D	85. C	117. D
22. C	54. A	86. B	118. D
23. D	55. D	87. C	119. B
24. B	56. B	88. B	120. B
25. A	57. D	89. D	121. B
26. C	58. B	90. A	122. B
27. B	59. D	91. C	123. A
28. D	60. A	92. D	124. D
29. D	61. B	93. D	125. A
30. C	62. C	94. B	
31. D	63. B	95. C	
32. C	64. A	96. D	

TEACHER CERTIFICATION STUDY GUIDE

Rigor Table

	Easy %20	Average Rigor %40	Rigorous %40
Question #	3, 8, 9, 24, 26, 28, 31, 33, 34, 43, 56, 60, 64, 70, 71, 83, 87, 88, 92, 98, 100, 105, 108, 110, 122,	1, 2, 4, 5, 6, 10, 11, 13, 14, 15, 19, 20, 27, 29, 30, 32, 38, 39, 40, 45, 47, 48, 50, 52, 54, 57, 65, 67, 72, 77, 78, 79, 82, 84, 90, 93, 94, 96, 97, 99, 102, 103, 106, 109, 111, 113, 115, 117, 121, 124, 125	7, 12, 16, 17, 18, 21, 22, 23, 25, 35, 36, 37, 41, 42, 44, 46, 49, 51, 53, 55, 58, 59, 61, 62, 63, 66, 68, 69, 73, 74, 75, 76, 80, 81, 85, 86, 89, 91, 95, 101, 104, 107, 112, 114, 116, 118, 119, 120, 123,

TEACHER CERTIFICATION STUDY GUIDE

Rationales with Sample Questions

1. A school library media specialist is searching for ways to make the school library more effective. Which of the following would not be a successful strategy?
   (Skill 1.1) Rigorous

   a. The school library media specialist develops activities that help to develop creativity and support critical thinking skills.
   b. The school library media specialist works in isolation to plan effective programs that support curriculum guidelines.
   c. The school library media specialist develops activities to expand students' interests and promote lifelong learning.
   d. The school library media specialist provides physical access to resources.

   Answer: b. The school library media specialist works in isolation to plan effective programs that support curriculum guidelines.

   For a media program to be most effective, the media specialist should work closely with classroom teachers to form a strong collaborative partnership. While a media specialist may have to work in isolation to plan effective programs, it is not the most desired result. This makes Option B the most appropriate answer.

2. A statement defining the core principles of a school library media program is called the:
   (Skill 1.2) Average rigor

   a. mission
   b. policy
   c. procedure
   d. objective

   Answer: a. mission

   The core principles of an organization are outlined in a mission statement. An objective is a specific statement of measurable result that reflects the mission statement.

TEACHER CERTIFICATION STUDY GUIDE

3. **Which version of *Information Power* was published in 1998?**
   (Skill 1.2) Easy

   a. *Information Power: The Role of the School Library Media Program*
   b. *Information Power: A Review of Research*
   c. *Information Power: Guidelines for School Library Media Programs*
   d. *Information Power: Building Partnerships for Learning*

Answer: d. *Information Power: Building Partnerships for Learning*

Option D is the version that was published in 1998. *Information Power: Guidelines for School Library Media Programs* was published in 1988.

4. **The school library media center should be an inviting space that encourages learning. To accomplish this the school library media specialist should do all of the following except:**
   (Skill 1.3) Average rigor

   a. collaborate with school staff and students.
   b. create a schedule where each class comes to the media center each eek for instruction.
   c. arrange materials so that they are easy to locate.
   d. promote the program as a wonderful place for learning.

Answer: b. create a schedule where each class comes to the media center each week for instruction

The goal of a school library is to operate under a flexible schedule to maximize use of the media center and its resources. This makes Option B the most appropriate answer.

5. **All of the following organizations serve school libraries except:**
   (Skill 1.4) Average rigor

   a. AASL
   b. AECT
   c. ALCT
   d. ALA

Answer: c. ALCT

The American Association of School Librarians (AASL), The Association for Educational Communications and Technology (AECT), and the American Library Association (ALA) are all organizations that support and serve school libraries.

6. According to the AASL-AECT national guidelines, which of the following is NOT one of the three overlapping roles of the school library media specialist?
   (Skill 1.4) Average rigor

   a. information specialist.
   b. equipment technician.
   c. teacher.
   d. instructional consultant.

Answer: b. equipment technician

While a library media specialist must serve as information specialist to promote information literacy, as instructional consultant when collaborating with teachers to design instructional resources, and teacher, their responsibilities do not include equipment technician.

7. According to AASL/AECT guidelines, in his or her role as *instructional consultant*, the school library media specialist uses his or her expertise to:
   (Skill 1.4) Rigorous

   a. assist teachers in acquiring information skills which they can incorporate into classroom instruction.
   b. provide access to resource sharing systems.
   c. plan lessons in media production.
   d. provide staff development activities in equipment use.

Answer: d. provide staff development activities in equipment use.

As an instructional consultant, the school library media specialist does provide staff development activities. Providing access is part of the role of program administrator. Assisting teachers and planning lessons is part of the teaching role of a media specialist. This makes Option D the most appropriate answer

8. **QCC is the acronym for:**
   (Skill 1.5) Easy

   a. Quality Curriculum Content
   b. Quality Classroom Curriculum
   c. Quality Core Curriculum
   d. Quality Classroom Content

Answer: c. Quality Core Curriculum

The curriculum standards for Georgia are often referred to as QCC or Quality Core Curriculum.

9. **For students to take responsibility for their own learning the media specialist much teach them all of the following but:** *(Skill 1.6) Easy*

   a. locate resources.
   b. evaluate resources.
   c. purchase resources
   d. use resources.

Answer: c. purchase resources

For students to be information literate they should know how to find, evaluation and use resources. It is not necessary for students to know to purchase materials.

10. **When evaluating resources for effectiveness it is important to consider all of the following except:**
    (Skill 2.1) Average rigor

    a. style of the web page.
    b. the intended audience.
    c. whether or not the site is from a scholarly source.
    d. the scope of the information

Answer: a. style of the web page

The style of the web page is not as important as the audience, whether or not the site is a scholarly source, or the scope of the information. This makes Option A the most appropriate answer.

11. A periodical index search which allows the user to pair Keywords with <u>and</u>, <u>but</u>, or <u>or</u> is called
    (Skill 2.1) Average rigor

    a. Boolean.
    b. dialoguing.
    c. wildcarding.
    d. truncation.

Answer: a. Boolean

The most appropriate answer is Option A, Boolean. A Boolean search uses keywords along with terms such as and, but, and or, to define the search. Wildcarding is a form of searching that uses something such as an asterisks to find different formats of words or terms.

12. When a new media specialist comes to a library, it is important for them to become familiar with the existing resource collection. One of the best ways to do this is to:
    (Skill 2.2) Rigorous

    a. consult the district director regarding collection policies.
    b. browse the shelves to evaluate what is available.
    c. examine collections of other comparable schools.
    d. study the school's curriculum to understand the needs of users.

Answer: b. browse the shelves to evaluate what is available

The most effective way for a media specialist to get to know their media collection is to browse the shelves. The other options may be helpful in determining the overall media program. Option B is the most appropriate answer.

TEACHER CERTIFICATION STUDY GUIDE

13. Which of the following is the least effective way of communicating school library media policies, procedures and rules to media center patrons?
    (Skill 2.5) Average rigor

a. announcements made in faculty and parent support group meetings.
b. a published faculty procedures manual.
c. written guidelines in the student handbook or special media handbill.
d. a videotape orientation viewed over the school's closed circuit television system.

Answer: a. announcements made in faculty and parent support group meetings.

When providing information regarding policies, procedures and rules for media center patrons it is important to provide them with tangible and detailed information. With Option A, announcements at meetings, the information is not necessarily written down and the media specialist may have to rely on those present to share information with others. It is the least reliable.

14. A library procedures manual should contain which of the following?
    (Skill 2.3) Average rigor

a. mission
b. specific media policies
c. specific media procedures
d. all of the above

Answer: d. all of the above

A library procedures manual should contain the mission statement for the media program, policies (including collection development, acceptable use, circulation, etc.) and procedures for various tasks. Option D is the most appropriate answer.

TEACHER CERTIFICATION STUDY GUIDE

15. All but which of the following criteria are used when determining fair use of copyrighted material for classroom use?
    (Skill 2.4) Average rigor

    a. Brevity Test.
    b. Spontaneity Test.
    c. Time Test.
    d. Cumulative Effect Test.

Answer: c. Time Test

Copyrighted materials used in a classroom must pass the criteria under the brevity, spontaneity, and cumulative effect tests in order to fall under the fair use guidelines.

16. Section 108 of the Copyright Act permits the copying of an entire book if three conditions are met. Which of the following is NOT one of those conditions?
    (Skill 2.4) Rigorous

    a. The library intends to allow inter-library loan of the book.
    b. The library is an archival library.
    c. The copyright notice appears on all the copies.
    d. The library is a public library.

Answer: a. The library intends to allow inter-library loan of the book.

Section 108 does allow a library to make a single copy of a book for archival purposes. It does not cover books that are to be copied and used for inter-library loans.

17. Under the copyright brevity test, an educator may reproduce without written permission
    (Skill 2.4) Rigorous

    a. 10% of any prose or poetry work.
    b. 500 words from a 5000 word article.
    c. 240 words of a 2400 word story.
    d. no work over 2500 words.

Answer: b. 500 words from a 5000 word article.

Under the brevity test up to 250 words of a poem can be copied providing it is under 2 pages. An article of 2500 words or less can be copied entirely. Ten percent of an article over 2500 words can be used making Option B the most appropriate answer

MEDIA SPECIALIST

18. "Fair Use" policy in videotaping off-air from commercial television requires the instructor to:
    (Skill 2.4) Rigorous

a. show in 5 days, erase by the 20th day.
b. show in 10 days, erase by the 30th day.
c. show in 10 days, erase by the 45th day.
d. no restrictions.

Answer: c. show in 10 days, erase by the 45th day.

Fair Use Guidelines for recorded videotapes for nonprofit educational institutions state that the recording must be shown within 10 days and must be erased by the 45th day.

19. Licensing has become a popular means of copyright protection in the area of
    (Skill 2.4) Average rigor

a. duplicating books for interlibrary loan.
b. use of software application on multiple machines.
c. music copying.
d. making transparency copies of books or workbooks that are too expensive to purchase.

Answer: b. use of software application on multiple machines.

When purchasing software the customer will generally received either a CD-ROM or DVD for installation purposes. The most important piece of packaging or file included on the software is the license. The license(s) purchased determine the number of computers in which the software can be loaded. Installing the software on more than the number listed on the license violated copyright and can result in a lawsuit by the publisher

20. Which of the following is a file extension for a video file?
    (Skill 2.5) Average rigor

a. .mp3
b. .wav
c. .avi
d. .jpeg

Answer: c. .avi

One format for video files is the .avi. The .mp3 and .wav files are audio files. The .jpeg format is for picture files.

MEDIA SPECIALIST

21. Which writer composes young adult literature in the fantasy genre?
(Skill 3.1) Rigorous

a. Stephen King.
b. Piers Anthony.
c. Virginia Hamilton.
d. Phyllis Whitney.

Answer: b. Piers Anthony

Piers Anthony is the author of such books as *Ghost*, *Firefly*, and *Bio of an Ogre*. He is the only author listed that writes fantasy for young adults.

22. Which fiction genre do authors Isaac Asimov, Louise Lawrence and Andre Norton represent?
(Skill 3.1) Rigorous

a. adventure.
b. romance.
c. science fiction.
d. fantasy.

Answer: c. science fiction.

All of these authors represent Option C, science fiction titles for each include:
Asimov- *I Robot, Foundation Trilogy*
Lawrence – *Children of the Dust, Moonwind*
Norton – *Stargate, Android at Arms*

23. All of the following are authors of young adult fiction EXCEPT
(Skill 3.1) Rigorous

a. Paul Zindel.
b. Norma Fox Mazer.
c. S.E. Hinton.
d. Maurice Sendak

Answer: d. Maurice Sendak

Maurice Sendak is best known for his picture books for young children such as *Where the Wild Things Are*.

24. The award given for the best children's literature (text) is:
    (Skill 3.1) Easy

    a. the Caldecott.
    b. the Newbery.
    c. the Pulitzer.
    d. the Booklist.

Answer: b. the Newbery

Option B, the Newberry Award, is the award give to an outstanding children's book. It was named for bookseller John Newbery, who was the first to publish literature for children in the second half of 18th century England. While the Caldecott Award does recognize children's literature, this award is for outstanding illustrators.

25. Which book was selected as the Georgia Book Award Winner for the picture book category in 2004-05?
    (Skill 3.1) Rigorous

    a. *Stanley's Party* by Linda Bailey and Bill Slavin
    b. *Bark, George* by Jules Feiffer
    c. *No, David* by David Shannon
    d. *Loser* by Jerry Spinelli

Answer: a. *Stanley's Party* by Linda Bailey and Bill Slavin

The correct answer is Option A, *Stanley's Party*. Option B is the 2001-2002 winner for picture books. Option C is the 1999-2000 winner. Option D is the 2004-05 middle grades winner.

26. To foster the collaborative process the media specialist must possess all of the following skills except:
    (Skill 3.2) Easy

    a. leadership
    b. flexibility
    c. perverse
    d. persistence

Answer: c. perverse

A school library media specialist must be flexible, possess good leadership skills, and be persistent making Option C the most appropriate response.

27. The role of the Media Committee or Media Advisory Committee is to assist with all of the following except:
    (Skill 3.2) Average rigor

    a. determine program direction
    b. evaluate the media specialist
    c. direct budget decisions
    d. collaborate with the media specialist

    Answer: b. evaluate the media specialist

    The Media Advisory Committee has the responsibility of helping to determine essential elements of the media collection, but they do not evaluate the media specialist.

28. When selecting books for students in grades k-2, it is best to choose books with which of the following characteristics?
    (Skill 3.3) Easy

    a. strong picture support
    b. familiar language patterns
    c. utilize cuing systems
    d. all of the above

    Answer: d. all of the above

    The best answer is Option D. Young readers need books that have strong picture support, repetitive language patterns, and strong cuing systems.

29. *The Horn Book* is
    (Skill 3.4) Average rigor

    a. a book about trumpets
    b. a children's picture book
    c. a professional journal
    d. a source for resource reviews

    Answer: d. a source for resource reviews

    The Horn Book is a collective review resource that lists book reviews as well as listing additional places where the item has been reviewed. While it is a professional resource, it is not a professional journal. This makes Option D the most appropriate answer.

30. Which of these publications does not contain reviews for various types of publications:
    (Skill 3.4) Average rigor

    a. School Library Journal
    b. Booklist
    c. Media Center Review
    d. The Horn Book

Answer: c. Media Center Review

The best answer is c, Media Center Review. All of the other publications provide reviews for books and other resources.

31. Literature appreciation activities can include which of the following:
    (Skill 3.5) Easy

    a. author studies
    b. genre studies
    c. book talks
    d. all of the above

Answer: d. all of the above

Literature appreciation activities can include: author studies, book talks, genre studies, among other activities. That makes Option D the most appropriate answer.

32. Factors that influence the atmosphere of a library media center contain all of the following except:
    (Skill 4.1) Average rigor

    a. aesthetic appearance
    b. acoustical ceiling and floor coverings.
    c. size of the media center
    d. proximity to classrooms

Answer: c. size of the media center

While the size of the media center is important, it does not necessarily have a bearing on the atmosphere. This makes Option C the most appropriate answer.

33. ***Information Power: Building Partnerships for Learning*** recommends flexible scheduling for
    (Skill 4.2) Easy

    a. elementary school library media centers.
    b. middle school library media centers.
    c. secondary school library media centers.
    d. all school library media centers.

Answer: d. all school library media centers.

Flexible access to resources is conducive to encouraging just–in–time learning. Resources are available at the point of need. Collaboration with classroom teachers makes flexible access even more effective. Thus all of the school library media centers should follow a flexible schedule making Option D the most appropriate answer

34. **When creating a schedule for a school library media center the type of schedule that maximizes access to resources is a:**
    (Skill 4.2) Easy

    a. fixed schedule
    b. open schedule
    c. partial fixed schedule
    d. flexible schedule

Answer: d. flexible schedule

The best answer is d, flexible schedule. A flexible schedule allows students to have access to resources at the point of need. It maximizes the use of resources and allows media specialists to be accessible for collaborative planning with teachers.

35. Contemporary library media design models should consider which of the following an optional need?
    (Skill 4.3) Rigorous

    a. flexibility of space to allow for reading, viewing, and listening.
    b. space for large group activities such as district meetings, standardized testing, and lectures.
    c. traffic flow patterns for entrance and exit from the media center as well as easy movement within the center.
    d. adequate and easy to rearrange storage areas for the variety of media formats and packaging style of modern materials.

Answer: b. space for large group activities such as district meetings, standardized testing, and lectures.

Flexibility of space, traffic flow patterns that allow ease of movement, and adequate storage are all crucial to design of a media center. Therefore, Option B is the best answer. While a space for large group activities is desirable for community use, it is not vital to the operation of a school library media center.

36. The most important consideration in the design of a new school library media center is
    (Skill 4.3) Rigorous

    a. the goals of the library media center program.
    b. the location of the facility on the school campus.
    c. state standards for facilities use.
    d. the demands of current technologies.

Answer: a. the goals of the library media center program

The goals of a library media program should be a most important consideration when planning a new school media center. The other options should be considered, but Option A is the most appropriate answer.

TEACHER CERTIFICATION STUDY GUIDE

37. **The ADA Accessibility Guidelines for Buildings and Facilities recommends that a media center allows *how much aisle space*?**
    (Skill 4.3) Rigorous

    a. 41 inches
    b. 42 inches
    c. 43 inches
    d. 44 inches

    Answer: b. 42 inches

    ADA guidelines specify and aisle width of 42 inches making Option B the most appropriate answer.

38. **Key design elements to consider when renovating or building a new facility include:**
    (Skill 4.4) Average rigor

    a. Traffic flow
    b. Access for physically impaired users
    c. Security needs
    d. all of the above

    Answer: d. all of the above

    Whether planning for a new media center or renovating an existing one there are many things that need to be taken into consideration. Among the considerations are the traffic flow, plans for access for impaired users and security. Other considerations would be appropriate space for specific tasks and furniture height. This makes Option D the most appropriate answer.

39. **A cooperative relationship between a media specialist and a teacher is known as:**
    (Skill 4.5) Average rigor

    a. collection development
    b. collaboration
    c. telecommunications
    d. flexible scheduling

    Answer: b. collaboration

    The most appropriate answer is Option B. The cooperative relationship between a media specialist and a teacher is known as collaboration.

40. Which of the following is an example of quantitative data that would be used to evaluate a school library media program?
    (Skill 4.6) Average rigor

    a. Personnel evaluations
    b. Usage statistics
    c. Surveys
    d. Interviews

Answer b. Usage statistics

Option B is the most appropriate answer because it is the only one listed that provides measurable data. All of the others are qualitative forms of data.

41. An accredited elementary school has maintained an acceptable number of items in its print collection for ten years. In the evaluation review, this fact is evidence of both
    (Skill 4.6) Rigorous

    a. diagnostic and projective standards.
    b. diagnostic and quantitative standards.
    c. projective and quantitative standards.
    d. projective and qualitative standards.

Answer: b. diagnostic and quantitative standards.

Diagnostic evaluations are standards based on conditions existing in programs that have already been judged excellent. The acceptable print collection can be compared to national guidelines for diagnostic information. Quantitative evaluations involve numerical data of some kind. By taking a look at the numbers in the collection the media specialist can review collection totals. Option B is the correct answer.

42. The principal is completing the annual report. He or she needs to include substantive data on use of the media center. In addition to the number of book circulations, he or she would like to know the proportionate use of the media center's facilities and services by the various grade levels or content areas. This information can most quickly be obtained from:
(Skill 4.6) Rigorous

a. the class scheduling log.
b. student surveys.
c. lesson plans.
d. inventory figures.

Answer: a. the class scheduling log

One of the best tools to use to determine how the media center's facilities are being used is the schedule. Often the schedule is broken down by the various areas in the media center. Teachers may schedule the specific area(s) they need. This makes Option A the most appropriate answer.

43. The ACLU's mission is to preserve First Amendment rights for all Americans. ACLU is the acronym for which organization:
(Skill 4.7) Easy

a. American Curricular Libraries Union
b. American Civil Libraries Union
c. American Civil Liberties Union
d. American Curricular Liberties Union

Answer: c. American Civil Liberties Union

The most appropriate answer is Option C. The American Civil Liberties Union is known by the acronym, ACLU.

44. **In the landmark U.S. Supreme Court ruling in favor of Pico, the court's opinion established that**
    (Skill 4.7) Rigorous

   a. library books, being optional not required reading, could not be arbitrarily removed by school boards.
   b. school boards have the same jurisdiction over library books as they have over textbooks.
   c. the intent to remove pervasively vulgar material is the same as the intent to deny free access to ideas.
   d. First Amendment challenges in regards to library books are the responsibility of appeals courts.

Answer: a. library books, being optional not required reading, could not be arbitrarily removed by school boards.

In the Supreme Court Case: Board of Education, Island Trees Union Free School District No. 26 v. Pico states that library books, being optional not required reading, could not be arbitrarily removed by school boards

45. **The two main categories of print resources found in most libraries are:**
    (Skill 5.1, 14.1) Average rigor

   a. reference and circulating materials
   b. picture books and chapter books
   c. reference books and picture books
   d. encyclopedias and chapter books

Answer: a reference and circulating materials

Materials in a media collection are generally found under two main headings, reference and circulating materials. Reference materials normally stay in the media center or are reserved under special check-out. Circulating materials are all of those that are checked out for patron use.

46. What is one advantage of keeping print resources in a media collection?
    (Skill 5.2) Rigorous

a   Information is easier to find in print resources.
b. Young children need to learn how to "use" a book.
c. Print materials last a long time.
d. Print materials are interactive

Answer: b. Young children need to learn how to "use" a book.

It is important for young children to learn how to handle a book. They need understand the basics of front and back covers, title page, etc. The most appropriate answer is Option B.

47. A search that uses specific terms to locate information is called a:
    (Skill 5.3) Average rigor

a. reference search
b. keyword search
c. ready reference search
d. operator search

Answer: b. keyword search

A keyword search uses specific terms to locate information. The most appropriate answer is Option B.

48. Which of the following searches would most likely return the most results?
    (Skill 5.4) Average rigor

a. lions AND tigers
b. lions NOT tigers
c. lions OR tigers
d. lions AND NOT tigers

Answer: c. lions OR tigers

The use of OR in the search lets the search engine know to find articles that contain either of the words listed. With the use of AND, the search engine will look for articles that have both words in the article.

TEACHER CERTIFICATION STUDY GUIDE

49. A request from a social studies class for the creation of a list of historical fiction titles for a book report assignment is a _____ request.
    (Skill 5.5) Rigorous

    a. ready reference.
    b. research.
    c. specific needs.
    d. complex search.

Answer: c. specific needs.

Requests made for particular titles or resources are known as a special needs request. Option C is the most appropriate answer.

50. All of the following are periodical directories except:
    (Skill 5.5) Average rigor

    a. *Ulrich's*
    b. *TNYT*
    c. *SIRS*
    d. *PAIS*

Answer: b. TNYT

TNYT is the acronym for The New York Times. It is the only one of the four that is not a periodical directory. This makes the most appropriate answer Option B.

51. When evaluating resources for effectiveness it is important to consider all of the following except:
    (Skill 6.1) Rigorous

    a. style of the web page.
    b. the intended audience.
    c. whether or not the site is from a scholarly source.
    d. the scope of the information

Answer: a. style of the web page

The style of the web page is not as important as the audience, whether or not the site is a scholarly source, or the scope of the information. This makes Option A the most appropriate answer.

MEDIA SPECIALIST

TEACHER CERTIFICATION STUDY GUIDE

52. **In most learning hierarchies, which of the following is the lowest order critical thinking skill?**
    (Skill 6.2) Average rigor

    a. appreciation.
    b. inference.
    c. recall.
    d. comprehension

Answer: c. recall

The lowest of the critical thinking skills is recall. Recall the basic facts of stories, dates, and events. This makes the most appropriate answer Option C.

53. **After reading *The Pearl,* a tenth grader asks, "Why can't we start sentences with *and* like John Steinbeck?" This student is showing the ability to**
    (Skill 6.2) Rigorous

    a. appreciate.
    b. comprehend.
    c. infer.
    d. evaluate.

Answer: d. evaluate.

Under the description of the Bloom's Taxonomy level of evaluation students that demonstrate this level of higher order thinking are able to :
- Make choices based upon well thought out arguments
- Compare ideas
- And recognize subjectivity

54. **In most learning hierarchies, which of the following is the highest order critical thinking skill?**
    (Skill 6.2) Average rigor

    a. appreciation.
    b. inference.
    c. recall.
    d. comprehension.

Answer: a. appreciation

In order of difficulty recall is the lowest critical thinking skill, followed by inference then comprehension and appreciation. Appreciation would be the highest level skill in this list making Option A the most appropriate answer.

55. In the production of a teacher/student made audio-visual material, which of the following is NOT a factor in the planning phase? *(Skill 6.3) Rigorous*

a. stating the objectives.
b. analyzing the audience.
c. determining the purpose.
d. selecting the format.

Answer: d. selecting the format.
During the planning phase it is necessary to determine who the information is designed for. The determining of the format comes later.

56. Which of the following formats is best for large group presentations? *(Skill 6.4) Easy*

a. manipulatives
b. multimedia
c. audio recordings
d. photographs

Answer: b. multimedia

Multimedia presentations are most appropriate for large groups. When used in conjunction with projectors and large screens, multimedia presentations are very effective.

57. All of the following formats are best for small group learning except: *(Skill 6.4) Average rigor*

a. manipulatives
b. computer projection
c. photographs
d. computer software

Answer: d. computer software

Computer software used on a single machine is most appropriate for small groups. The most appropriate answer is Option D.

58. Which of the following is a popular format for citing resources?
    (Skill 6.5) Rigorous

    a. CMA
    b. APA
    c. DMA
    d. MPA

Answer: b. APA

One popular format for citing resources is the APA (American Psychological Association) style. Other popular formats include Modern Language Association (MLA) and the Chicago Manual of Style.

59. MLA style is a popular format for citing resources in a bibliography. MLA is the acronym for:
    (Skill 6.5) Rigorous

    a. Media Library Association
    b. Modern Library Association
    c. Modern Literary Association
    d. Modern Language Association

Answer: d. Modern Language Association

MLA format is a popular format for citing resources. The acronym stands for Modern Language Association.

60. A scoring guide that is generally subjective and contains specific criteria in which projects should be judged is known as a:
    (Skill 6.6) Easy

    a. rubric
    b. outline
    c. criteria
    d. evaluation

Answer: a. rubric

Rubrics are popular grading scales that can be used for product based assessments. Rubrics generally provide criteria that is based on a specific rating scale. Grades are determined by how closely the student has met the criteria.

61. As instructors, school library media specialists as instructors must be able to construct statements of objectives for instructional purposes. Which of the following is a properly stated objective?
(Skill 7.1) Rigorous

a. To describe the process necessary to locate books on Third World countries in the reference area.
b. To demonstrate the use of the library's automated catalog to aid a newcomer in determining whether a particular title is available.
c. To understand how the Dewey Decimal System works.
d. To identify ten authors who have contributed to economic, social, or cultural changes in the 20th century.

Answer: b. To demonstrate the use of the library's automated catalog to aid a newcomer in determining whether a particular title is available.

Instructional objectives are specific statements of a measurable result that will occur by a particular time, i.e., it must specify the conditions and criteria to be met effectively.

62. When working with patrons to determine their specific information needs it may be necessary to ask the patron a series of questions that uncover needs, often called a:
(Skill 7.2) Rigorous

a. ready reference request
b. special needs request
c. reference interview
d evaluation interview

Answer: c. reference interview

A reference interview may be necessary to determine the specific needs of the patron. A reference interview consists of asking the patron a series of open-ended questions that assist in narrowing the topic. This makes Option C the most appropriate answer.

TEACHER CERTIFICATION STUDY GUIDE

63. **Which of the following would be a good question to ask during a reference interview?**
    (Skill 7.2) Rigorous

    a. Do you have a topic?
    b. What is your topic?
    c. Have you located any resources regarding your topic?
    d. Do you know where to go to find the information?

    Answer: b. What is your topic?

    The most appropriate reference interview questions are open-ended making Option B the most appropriate answer. It is the only question that requires more than a yes or no answer.

64. **Howard Gardner is responsible for the creation of**
    (Skill 7.3) Easy

    a. Multiple Intelligences
    b. Taxonomies of Learning
    c. Big 6 Model
    d. @ Your Library

    Answer: a. Multiple Intelligences

    Howard Gardner is the creator of Multiple Intelligences. His theory stresses that each person has strengths is specific areas and that there are specific activities that will increase those strengths.

65. **Which of the following would be an example of an activity that would use the Bloom's taxonomy level of Recall or Knowledge?**
    (Skill 7.3) Average rigor

    a. Producing a presentation.
    b. Retelling a story.
    c. Rewriting the ending of a story.
    d. React to the author's language or style.

    Answer: b. Retelling a story.

    The recall or knowledge level of Bloom's focuses upon the repetition of facts. This makes Option B the most appropriate answer. All of the others require students to use higher order skills to accomplish the task.

66. **Authentic learning activities have students explore curricular objectives in the context of real world problems and projects. Which of the following is not an example of this type of activity?**
(Skill 7.4) Rigorous

a. Students create a brochure to make people aware of the needs of the community's food bank.
b. Students help the school create advertisements for an upcoming school event.
c. Students research a character found in a book they've read.
d. Students monitor and report on the water quality of a local pond or lake.

Answer: c. Students research a character found in a book they've read.

Authentic learning can be described as a process that has students explore curricular objectives within the context of real world problems. Researching a character from a book is not a real world issue. Therefore, Option C is the best answer.

67. **Skills that provide students with the ability to solve problems are known as**
(Skill 7.5) Average rigor

a. critical thinking skills
b. multiple intelligences
c. Loertscher's Taxonomies
d. authentic learning

Answer: a. critical thinking skills

Critical thinking skills are the skills students need to find solutions to complex problems. This makes Option A the most appropriate answer.

68. **When creating instructional materials which of the following is not a part of the planning phase?**
(Skill 7.6) Rigorous

a. determining the goal or objectives to be covered
b. creating the media
c. analyzing the audience
d. determining the purpose

Answer: b. create the media

Creating the media is part of the design phase while the others are key parts of the planning phase.

69. Collaboration between the media specialist and classroom teacher is the key to an effective library media program. Which of the following scenarios best describes a media specialist willing to foster a collaborative partnership with a teacher?
    (Skill 8.1) Rigorous

a. The media specialist meets only when approached by a classroom teacher who is asking for help.
b. The media specialist can only meet on Tuesdays and Thursdays from 1-2 due to the fixed schedule that has been set up for the media center.
c. The media specialist touches base with teachers on a regular basis and attends grade level planning sessions.
d. The media specialist only meets with teachers on each grade level who are interested in working collaboratively.

Answer: b. The media specialist can only meet on Tuesdays and Thursdays from 1-2 due to the fixed schedule that has been set up for the media center.

A flexible schedule is most conducive to fostering the collaborative process with teachers. When a media specialist is on a fixed schedule and only has a limited time each week to plan with teachers, the media specialist loses some of their effectiveness. Option B is the most appropriate answer.

70. Media specialists can assist teachers with the teaching of reading by assessing students' reading habits. Tools that can be used to accomplish this task include:
    (Skill 8.2) Easy

a. interviews
b. surveys
c. packaged assessment programs
d. all of the above

Answer: d. all of the above

When helping students make independent reading choices having a knowledge of student interests is very helpful. Interviews, surveys, and packaged assessments are all ways that interests can be determined.

TEACHER CERTIFICATION STUDY GUIDE

71. **As much as possible, information skills should be taught as**
    (Skill 8.3) Easy

    a. lessons independent of content studies.
    b. lessons to supplement content studies.
    c. lessons integrated into content studies.
    d. lessons enriched by content studies.

Answer: C. lessons integrated into content studies.

Georgia State Standards no longer include a separate technology section. Technology skills are included in core content area objectives. Option C is the most appropriate answer. Lessons are to be integrated into content studies.

72. **The creators of the Big 6 Model are:**
    (Skill 8.3) Average rigor

    a. Eisenberg and Berkowitz.
    b. Marzano and Bloom.
    c. Bloom and Gardner.
    d. Lance and Eisenberg.

Answer: a. Eisenberg and Berkowitz

The correct answer is Option A. Mike Eisenberg and Bob Berkowitz are the creators of the Big 6 Model for developing Information Literacy Skills.

73. **The capability to understand when information is needed and to identify, evaluate, and use the information effectively is known as:**
    (Skill 8.3) Rigorous

    a. Collaborative partnership
    b. Information literacy
    c. Taxonomies of literacy
    d. Bloom's Taxonomies

Answer: b. Information literacy

For students to be productive 21st century citizens it is important for them to be information literate. Students who are information literate can locate and use information effectively. The best answer for this question is Option B.

MEDIA SPECIALIST

TEACHER CERTIFICATION STUDY GUIDE

74. **Steps in the Big6 Model include all of the following except:**
    (Skill 8.3) Rigorous

    a. information seeking strategies
    b. location and access
    c. creation of information
    d. task definition

    Answer: c. creation of information

    Creation of information is the only option that is not included in the Big6 Information Literacy model. Option C is the most appropriate answer.

75. **Another popular information literacy model is:**
    (Skill 8.3) Rigorous

    a. Bloom's Taxonomies
    b. Star Reader
    c. Pathways to Knowledge
    d. Follett Taxonomies

    Answer: c. Pathways to Knowledge

    Pathways to Knowledge is an information literacy model that closely follows the steps outlined in the Big 6 model. Option C is the most appropriate answer.

76. **Students with disabilities would benefit from specialized software that can read online text, PDF documents and scanned pages. One popular software title is called:**
    (Skill 8.4) Rigorous

    a. Kurzweil Reader
    b. Accelerated Reader
    c. Star Reader
    d. Kertfeld Reader

    Answer: a. Kurzweil Reader

    The Kurzweil Reader is software that assists students with disabilities. The software can read PDF documents and text online and scanned documents. It is a powerful tool for all students, not just those with disabilities.

77. The media specialist needs to expand the collection to include a wider variety of resources for visually impaired students. Which of the following would be least beneficial?
    (Skill 8.4) Average rigor

    a. Books with larger print.
    b. Books in Braille format.
    c. Books in audio format.
    d. Books in video format.

    Answer: d. Books in video format.

    Books in video format would be least beneficial. Students with visual impairments would have a more difficult time gaining information from this format than any of the other formats listed.

78. Web page editing software that allows the user to preview web pages as they are being created is called:
    (Skill 8.5) Average rigor

    a. WYSWYG
    b. WYSIYG
    c. WISWYG
    d. WYSIWYG

    Answer: d. WYSIWYG

    The correct answer is Option D. Web page editing software that allows users to preview web pages as they are being created is called WYSIWYG software or What You See Is What You Get.

79. Software designed to organize, manage and retrieve resources quickly and easily is called:
    (Skill 8.5) Average rigor

    a. database
    b. spreadsheet
    c. word processing
    d. teleconference

    Answer: a database

    Databases are used to organize, manage and retrieve resources quickly, making Option A the most appropriate answer. While spreadsheets are able to perform those tasks, their primary purpose is to perform calculations.

80. Software that allows users to communicate over the Internet using audio and/or video is called:
(Skill 8.5) Rigorous

a. database
b. spreadsheet
c. web editor
d. teleconferencing

Answer: d. teleconferencing

Teleconferencing software and equipment allows video and/ or audio to be broadcast online for the purpose of communicating with others. Option D is the most appropriate answer.

81. One key component of the National Board for Professional Teaching Standards for Library Media is self reflection. Which of the following is the best definition of self reflection?
(Skill 8.6) Rigorous

a. The process that guides one through examination of previous activities and helps one to propose improvements for the future.
b. The process that guides one through examination of current activities and helps one to propose improvements for past activities.
c. The process that guides one through examination of previous activities and helps one propose improvements for past activities.
d. The process that guides one through examination of future activities and helps one propose improvements for future activities.

Answer: a. The process that guides one through examination of previous activities and helps one to propose improvements for the future.

Option A is the most appropriate answer. Self reflection is a key component of the National Board Certification process and should be part of a teacher's daily practice. It is important to reflect upon lessons or activities and analyze what can be done to improve upon the activity for future reference.

82. **A general statement or outcome that is broken down into specific skills is known as a:**
    (Skill 9.1) Average rigor

a. policy
b. procedure
c. goal
d. objective

Answer: c. goal

A goal is a general statement or outcome that is broken down into specific measurable objectives. Option C is the most appropriate answer.

83. **When working to improve student instruction, the media specialist should work collaboratively with which groups?**
    (Skill 9.2) Easy

a. grade level
b. school curriculum committee
c. district curriculum committee
d. all of the above

Answer: d. all of the above

It is important for a media specialist to participate at all levels of curriculum development. They should take part in grade level planning meetings to form collaborative relationships with teachers. They should participate in school and district level curriculum committees in order to share their expertise in curriculum and better align their media program to curricular goals. It is also important for a media specialist to participate in state and national level organizations that affect library media programs.

TEACHER CERTIFICATION STUDY GUIDE

84. The media specialist is interested in beginning collaborative planning sessions with the teachers within the school, but not all of the teachers are interested. The media specialist should:
    (Skill 9.3) Average rigor

    a. wait until all of the teachers are interested
    b. have the principal make all teachers collaboratively plan with the media specialist
    c. work with the teachers who are most willing to engage in the process
    d. abandon the idea

Answer: c. work with the teachers who are most willing to engage in the process

A good place for media specialists to begin forming collaborative relationships is with those who are willing. As the media specialist gains confidence and support they need to branch out to meet with all teachers. Planning with teachers during grade level meetings is an ideal way to enhance the process.

85. The American Library Association defines four levels of collaboration. The four levels coordination, cooperation, integrated instruction and:
    (Skill 9.4) Rigorous

    a. cooperative grouping
    b. independent instruction
    c. integrated curriculum
    d. instructional partnership

Answer: c. integrated curriculum

The fourth level of collaboration as defined by ALA is integrated curriculum. At this stage technology has been seamlessly integrated into the entire curriculum. There is strong administrative support for this to occur at its fullest potential.

86. Collaborative partnerships with staff can take on many forms. All of the following are examples of partnerships except:
(Skill 9.5) Rigorous

a. serving on curriculum development committees
b. viewing the school's curriculum and creating lessons
c. assisting teachers in planning, designing, and teaching lessons
d. assisting teachers and students with the use of new technologies

Answer: b. viewing the school's curriculum and creating lessons

For the collaborative process to be effective the media specialist needs to work closely with the classroom teacher to create and plan lessons. The planning should not be conducted by the media specialist alone. This may occur, but it is not the desired result. Option B is the most appropriate answer.

87. The practice of examining the quantity and quality of the school library media resource collection which provides a "snapshot" of the collection is called:
(Skill 9.6) Easy

a. collection development
b. collection maintenance
c. collection mapping
d. weeding

Answer: c. collection mapping

Collection maps are of great benefit to the school library media specialist. They help to identify strengths and weaknesses in the collection, plan for purchases and identify areas in need of weeding. Option C is the most appropriate answer.

88. Current trends in school library media include all of the following except:
(Skill 10.1) Easy

a. use of Internet
b. face to face instruction
c. developing partnerships
d. use of electronic books

Answer: b. face to face instruction

Face to face instruction is not one of the current trends in school library media. All of the others represent some of the trends affecting school library media programs.

89. Two information literacy models are:
(Skill 10.2) Rigorous

a. Big6 and Bloom's
b. Bloom's and Loertscher
c. Loertscher and ISearch
d. Big 6 and ISearch

Answer: d. Big 6 and ISearch

Two popular information literacy models are the Big6 and ISearch. Option D is the most appropriate answer.

90. Staff development is most effective when it includes:
(Skill 10.3) Average rigor

a. continuing support
b. hand-outs
c. video tutorials
d. stated objectives

Answer: a. continuing support

While the other options are important to consider when providing staff development, it is the provision of continuing support that ensures the information learned will used to its fullest potential. Option A is the most appropriate answer.

91. Research that examines current teaching strategies and searches for ways to improve upon them is known as :
(Skill 10.4) Rigorous

a. quantitative research
b. qualitative research
c. action research
d. procedural research

Answer: c. action research

Action research is most often conducted in the midst of the teaching process. As teachers teach they examine the effectiveness of the lesson and look to improve there performance. The process is similar to that of self-reflection but may include a more detailed collection of data.

92. **A good leader should:**
    (Skill 11.1) Easy

    a. delegate responsibility
    b. show respect for colleagues
    c. engage in continuing education
    d. all of the above

Answer: d. all of the above

A good leader should strive to continuously improve their performance while building a great team to accomplish the desired goal. It is important that the demonstrate their quest to be a lifelong learner, respect their colleagues and learn to delegate responsibilities based upon the strengths of those around them.

93. **When implementing new technologies it is important for the media specialist to model its use. It is also important for the media specialist to:**
    (Skill 11.2) Average rigor

    a. Send updated hand-outs to staff.
    b. Provide web resources to assist with utilization of the tool.
    c. Provide brief refresher modules.
    d. All of the above.

Answer: d. all of the above

Staff are more responsive and tend to utilize new technologies more when they know they have support when they need it most. Option D is the most appropriate answer because all three play an important role in that process.

94. **Which of the following is an example of quantitative data that would be used to evaluate a school library media program?**
    (Skill 11.4) Average rigor

    a. Personnel evaluations
    b. Usage statistics
    c. Surveys
    d. Interviews

Answer b. Usage statistics

Option B is the most appropriate answer because it is the only one listed that provides measurable data. All of the others are qualitative forms of data.

95. Evaluation criteria that presents guidelines for conditions as they ought to be ideally is known as:
   (Skill 11.4)Rigorous

   a. diagnostic standards.
   b. quantitative standards.
   c. projective standards.
   d. qualitative standards.

Answer: c. projective standards

A wide variety of evaluation criteria may be used. The criteria may be:
1. Diagnostic. These are standards based on conditions existing in programs that have already been judged excellent.
2. Projective. These standards are guidelines for conditions as they ought to be ideally.
3. Quantitative. These standards require numerical measurement.
4. Qualitative. These standards are designed to express essentially the measured criteria as quantitative without exact numerical amounts

96. Lesson plans, personnel evaluations, surveys, conferences, and criterion-referenced or teacher made tests are forms of which standard
   (Skill 11.4) Average rigor

   a. diagnostic standards.
   b. quantitative standards.
   c. projective standards.
   d. qualitative standards.

Answer: d. qualitative standards

Qualitative standards are descriptive in nature. Alll of the items listed are forms of qualitative data. This makes Option D the most appropriate answer.

97. Which of the following is not a benefit of forming partnerships within the community?
    (Skill 11.5) Average rigor

    a. increased support for media program
    b. decline in media resources
    c. provide wide array of resources
    d. increase parental involvement

Answer: b. decline in media resources

By forming partnerships with outside agencies the media specialist can often increase the resources available for their patrons. Option B is the most appropriate answer because forming partnerships does not decrease media resources.

98. Partners for a school library media program may include:
    (Skills 11.5) Easy

    a. universities
    b. local businesses
    c. community organizations
    d. all of the above

Answer: d. all of the above

Universities, local businesses, and community organizations are all viable partners for a media program. Universities may provide additional training for staff or open their resource catalog for use by local school districts. Local businesses often donate funds, equipment or professional expertise to local schools. Community organizations work to turn students into strong community leaders by providing programs and awards.

99. A network allows which of the following to occur?
    (Skill 12.1) Average rigor

    a. sharing files.
    b. sharing printers.
    c. sharing software.
    d. all of the above

Answer: d. all of the above.

A network allows the sharing of files, printers, and software. This makes Option D the most appropriate response.

TEACHER CERTIFICATION STUDY GUIDE

100. The online virtual library for Georgia that was developed by the Board of Regents of the University System of Georgia is called: (Skill 12.1) *Easy*

a. GALILEO
b. GSLMA
c. GAIT
d. GSPRA

Answer: a. GALILEO

The university system of Georgia provides GALILEO as a source of information to Georgia residents. Access can be found in schools and at local public libraries.

101. School libraries may wish to form partnerships with outside organizations for all of the following reasons except: *(Skill 12.2) Rigorous*

a. narrow student learning experience.
b. diminish financial support for library or school projects.
c. eliminate the need for the school library media specialist to be involved in the community
d. none of the above

Answer: d. none of the above

Partnerships with outside entities can benefit school library media programs by:
- the location of additional programs or resources to expand student learning experience.
- gaining financial support for library or school projects.
- locating sites off campus where the library may hold special programs to support curricular needs.
- the school library media specialist becoming more involved in community improvement in support of the school.
- developing a greater knowledge of concerns and issues within the community as a whole and their impact on the school.

Option D is the most appropriate answer.

MEDIA SPECIALIST

102. A catalog that contains materials from several library collections is known as a
    (Skill 12.3) Average rigor

    a.   Shared Catalog.
    b.   Cooperative Catalog.
    c.   Union Catalog.
    d.   Universal Catalog.

Answer: c. Union Catalog

Option C is the most appropriate answer. A union catalog exists when various entities combine their resource lists so that they can be shown in one catalog. This is most often done throughout school districts or through partnerships with colleges and universities.

103. Resources can be shared within a small geographic location such as a school by the use of a:
    (Skill 12.4) Average rigor

    a.   SWN.
    b.   MAN.
    c.   LAN.
    d.   WAN.

Answer: c. LAN

A LAN or local area network allows users to share information within a small geographic area. The WAN or wide area network allows users to share information over a large geographic area.

104. Which professional journal is published by the American Association of School Librarians.
    (Skill 12.5) Rigorous

    a.   *School Library Media Research*
    b.   *Library Trends*
    c.   *Library Power*
    d.   *Voices of Youth Advocate*

Answer: a. *School Library Media Research*

The only journal listed that is published by the AASL is *School Library Media Research*. This makes Option A the most appropriate response.

105. IRA is the acronym for the:
(Skill 12.5) Easy

a. Interactive Reading Administration.
b. International Reading Administration.
c. International Reading Association.
d. Interactive Reading Association.

Answer: c. International Reading Association.

International Reading Association or IRA supports literacy and often partners with library associations.

106. Which of the following is NOT one of three general criteria for selection of all materials?
(Skill 13.1) Average rigor

a. authenticity.
b. appeal.
c. appropriateness.
d. allocation.

Answer: d. allocation

When selecting materials the school library generally looks for materials that have reliable information, appeal to students and are appropriate for the grade levels their program serves. Option D, allocation is not one of the criteria use to select materials

107. Collection development policies are developed to accomplish all of the following except
(Skill 13.1) Rigorous

a. guarantee users freedom to access information.
b. recognize the needs and interests of users.
c. coordinate selection criteria and budget concerns.
d. recognize rights of individuals or groups to challenge these policies.

Answer: c. coordinate selection criteria and budget concerns

The main goal of a collection development policy is to set guidelines and procedures that govern how resources are purchased and managed. It does not coordinate any criteria or address funding issues.

TEACHER CERTIFICATION STUDY GUIDE

108. **The process of discarding worn or outdated books and materials is known as:**
     (Skill 13.2) Easy

a. weeding.
b. inventory.
c. collection mapping.
d. eliminating.

Answer: a. weeding

Option A is the most appropriate answer. Outdated or worn books and materials need to be removed from the library collection. This process is known as weeding

109. **An acronym that is often used to remind media specialists of the steps to weeding a collection is:**
     (Skill 13.2) Average rigor

a. WEAR.
b. MUSTIE.
c. ABCD.
d. RIPPED.

Answer: b. MUSTIE.

The acronym, MUSTIE, is used to assist media specialists with the weeding process. It stands for: misleading, ugly, superseded, trivial, irrelevant, elsewhere. This makes Option B the most appropriate answer.

110. **MARC is the acronym for:**
     (Skill 13.3) Easy

a. Mobile Accessible Recorded Content
b. Machine Accessible Readable Content
c. Machine Readable Content
d. Mobile Accessible Readable Content

Answer: c. Machine Readable Content

Option C is the most appropriate answer. MARC is the acronym for Machine Readable Content. The MARC format is used in the cataloging of resources.

MEDIA SPECIALIST

111. **AACR2 is the acronym for:**
     (Skill 13.3) Average rigor

  a. Anglo-American Cataloging Rules Second Edition
  b. American Association of Cataloging Rules Second Edition
  c. American Association of Content Rules Second Edition
  d. Anglo-American Content Rules Second Edition

Answer: a. Anglo-American Cataloging Rules Second Edition

Option A is the most appropriate answer. AACR2 outlines specific rules that must be followed when cataloging items.

112. **All of the following are components of a circulation policy except:**
     (Skill 13.4) Rigorous

  a. loan period
  b. process for handling overdues
  c. limitations
  d. location to post borrower's name

Answer: d. location to post borrower's name

The location to post a borrower's name is not a part of a circulation policy. The policy should include the length of the loan period, how to handle overdues, and such limitations as the number of books that can be checked out at once.

113. **When automating a library catalog it is important to consider which of the following prior to set up?**
     (Skill 13.5) Average rigor

  a. technical requirements
  b. loan period
  c. patron limitations
  d. color of spine labels

Answer: a. technical requirements

Prior to establishing or upgrading an automated library catalog one of the most important considerations should be the technical requirements. Schools should examine their network infrastructure and individual computers to determine if it will support the systems.

TEACHER CERTIFICATION STUDY GUIDE

114. When determining a specific piece of equipment to purchase, the school library media specialist should first consult
    (Skill 14.2) *Rigorous*

    a. local vendors for a demonstration.
    b. reviews in technology periodicals.
    c. manufacturers' catalogs for specifications.
    d. the state bid list for price.

Answer: c. manufacturer's catalogs for specifications.

Before purchasing a piece of equipment it is important to determine whether a particular piece will perform the needed task. One of the best places to find this answer is Option C, manufacturer's catalogs. The other resources may be helpful, once the basic specifications have been checked.

115. When new technologies arrive at the school it is most important to:
    (Skill 14.3) *Average rigor*

    a. inventory the item
    b. catalog the item
    c. train teachers to use the item
    d. do nothing.

Answer: c. train the teachers to use the item

While inventorying and cataloging items are an important part of the record keeping process of media centers, it is most important that staff learn to use the equipment. Technology equipment is generally expensive, therefore to ensure money was spent appropriately training must be provided. This makes Option C the most appropriate answer.

116. The Position Statement on Flexible Scheduling was developed by :
    (Skill 14.4) *Rigorous*

    a. AASL
    b. ALA
    c. AECT
    d. SLMA

Answer: a. AASL

The American Association of School Librarians have issued the Position Statement on Flexible Scheduling. It recommends full integration of information skills into the curriculum. Option A is the most appropriate answer.

117. Which of the following should participate in the development of local policies and procedures:
(Skill 15.1) Average rigor

a. teacher
b. student
c. parents
d. all of the above

Answer: d. all of the above

Teachers, students and parents should play a role in the development of local policies and procedures. This ensures equity for all types of users and gains insight from differing viewpoints. Administrators and media specialists should also serve on such a committee.

118. According to research on promotion techniques and support for library media programs, their staunchest ally must be the
(Skill 15.2) Rigorous

a. teaching faculty.
b. student body.
c. district media supervisor.
d. school principal.

Answer: d. school principal

In order to make the necessary changes needed to make the school library media center the true learning center of the school the school library media specialist must have the full support of the principal. Moving to flexible scheduling and truly integrated learning can be a big adjustment. It is only with the vision and leadership of the school principal that any changes can occur.

119. **In a school with one full-time library media assistant (clerk), which of the following are responsibilities of the assistant?**
    (Skill 15.3) Rigorous

    a. selecting and ordering titles for the print collection.
    b. performing circulation tasks and processing new materials.
    c. inservicing teachers on the integration of media materials into the school curriculum.
    d. planning and implementing programs to involve parents and community.

Answer: b. performing circulation tasks and processing new materials.

Option B is the most appropriate answer. Circulation tasks and the processing of materials generally involve clerical duties. The other options are usually performed by a licensed media specialists.

120. **In formulating an estimated collection budget consider all of the following except**
    (Skill 15.4) Rigorous

    a. attrition by loss, damage, or age.
    b. the maximum cost of item replacement.
    c. the number of students served.
    d. the need for expansion to meet minimum guidelines.

Answer: b. the maximum cost of item replacement

The first consideration for formulating a collection budget is to determine whether or not the collection meets minimum guidelines. Then decide upon the funding needed to meet the guidelines. It is also important to allot funds to replace lost or worn items. Option B, the maximum cost of item replacement is not used in formulating a collection budget making it the most appropriate answer.

121. **The most appropriate means of obtaining extra funds for library media programs is**
    (Skill 15.5) Average rigor

    a. having candy sales.
    b. conducting book fairs.
    c. charging fines.
    d. soliciting donations.

Answer: b. conducting book fairs.

The most appropriate answer for this question is Option B, conducting book fairs. This keeps in line with the main focus of a school library media program, literacy.

122. **Long range plans should span how many years?**
    (Skill 16.1) Easy

    a. 2 – 4
    b. 3 – 5
    c. 5 – 10
    d. 10 – 15

Answer: b. 3-5

Long range plans should be developed to span from 3-5 years. It is important to record progress and plan periodic evaluations to determine which goals may need to be adjusted due to changing student populations and funding.

123. **The Georgia agencies that have worked together to align services and standards pertaining to media programs are:**
    (Skill 16.2) Rigorous

    a. Georgia Library Association and the Georgia Department of Education
    b. Georgia Library Association and Georgia Association for Instructional Technology
    c. Georgia Department of Education and Georgia Association of Instructional Technology
    d. Georgia Media Specialists Association and the Georgia Department of Education

Answer: a. Georgia Library Association and the Georgia Department of Education

These two entities work together to ensure media services and curriculum standards are aligned with one another.

124. **Policies that determine procedures for copyright laws and reproduction of materials are generally determined at which level:**
    (Skill 16.3) Average rigor

    a. grade level
    b. school level
    c. community level
    d. district level

Answer: d. District level

Policies regarding copyright and acceptable use of resources are generally created at the district level. Individual schools may adopt extra requirements, but the overall guidelines are set on a larger scale.

125. The most efficient method of assessing which students are users or non-users of the library media center is reviewing
    (Skill 16.4) Average rigor

a. patron circulation records.
b. needs assessment surveys of students.
c. monthly circulation statistics.
d. the accession book for the current year.

Answer: a. patron circulation records.

By reviewing circulation records the school library media specialists can quickly survey who is and isn't checking out materials making Option A the best answer. A needs assessment generally takes a good deal of time to complete. The monthly circulation records provide a snapshot of the number of books checked out during a specific period.

www.ingramcontent.com/pod-product-compliance
Lightning Source LLC
Chambersburg PA
CBHW080538300426
44111CB00017B/2792